Last Meals

The Final Suppers of Serial Killers and Murderers

Dylan Frost

Contents

96 - Robert Alton Harris

99 - Adolf Hitler

102 - H. H. Holmes

104 - Saddam Hussein

106 - Bobby Joe Long

107 - Peter Kürten

110 - William Little

112 - Daniel Lucas

114 - Rhonda Belle Martin

116 - Timothy McVeigh

117 - Peter Miniel

119 - John Glenn Moody

121 - Benito Mussolini

124 - Dennis Nilsen

132 - Marion Albert Pruett

134 - Ricky Ray Rector

136 - Paul Ezra Rhoades

138 - Danny Rolling

140 - John Martin Scripps

143 - Sean Sellers

146 - Tommy Lynn Sells

148 - Gary Carl Simmons

150 - Ruth Snyder

151 - Frank Spisak

153 - Joseph Stalin

157 - Gerald Stano

159 - Joseph Taborsky

161 - Karla Faye Tucker

163 - Robert Van Hook

165 - Chester Wicker

167 - Steven Michael Woods Jr

168 - Aileen Wuornos

INTRODUCTION

Is is a longstanding custom in the United States that a
condemned prisoner about to be executed is granted a last
meal. They can, within reason, choose one last special meal to
eat before they are put to death. There are variations but this
custom still prevails today. The last meal is by no means
exclusive to the United States. In parts of Asia condemned
prisoners are still granted a last meal. In Europe it was more
common though for a prisoner to be offered alcohol or perhaps
a cigar before their execution rather than food. Alcohol and
tobacco are not permitted as part of a last request if someone
is executed in the United States today. They can have food
though. Burgers, pizzas, lobster, cherry pie, whatever they
want (dependent on which jurisdiction they reside in).

Most of the famous last meal requests in modern true crime
reside in the United States because the other western nations
have long since abolished the death penalty. It is not quite true
that condemned prisoners can order whatever they want as a
last meal. Sometimes they are limited to what the prison chefs
can actually find or cook themselves. In Florida, the last meal
is not allowed to exceed $40 and must be procured locally. In
some states the budget for the last meal is even lower.

Generally though, the request of a condemned prisoner will
usually be catered to as long as it isn't too elaborate or rare -
although in some cases some very elaborate last meal requests
have been granted. It is unavoidably fascinating of course to
see what famous killers choose as their last ever meal on
planet Earth. In 2012, the journal Appetite published a study
of last meals by condemned prisoners in the United States
from 2002 to 2006. The average last meal came in at 2,756
calories but there were cases of a last meal clocking in at 7,000
calories. As we shall see, one last meal request clocked in at
30,000 calories.

70% of last meal requests ordered fried food. The most
popular beverage (alcohol is not usually permitted) was Coca-

Cola. 17% of last meal requests asked for Coca-Cola to drink. The most popular last meal request overall in the United States is cheeseburger and fries. The most popular dessert request is ice cream. 24% of last meal requests involve burgers and 22% of last meals contain steak. Vegetarian meals are very rare. It seems there aren't too many vegetarians on death row. As we shall see, among the things which are surprisingly popular when it comes to death row last meals are baked potatoes and fish. A large number of famous killers have requested seafood for their last meal.

Prisons in Texas abandoned the tradition of the last meal for condemned prisoners in 2011. There are a couple of reasons why they did this. The first was the fact that there were numerous documented cases of prisoners receiving a last meal but then being reprieved at the last minute. Prisons clearly got a bit tired of laying on last meals for prisoners who (thanks to appeals) were then not even executed anyway.

Another reason why lawmakers and prison officials in Texas dropped the last meal request was the convicted murderer Lawrence Russell Brewer. For his last meal in a Texas prison, the condemned Brewer requested chicken-fried steaks, one pound of barbecued meat, a triple-patty bacon cheeseburger, a meat-lover's pizza, three fajitas, an omelet, a bowl of okra, one pint of Blue Bell Ice Cream, some peanut-butter fudge with crushed peanuts and three root beers. However, when this feast finally arrived Brewer never actually ate a single bite of it. As you might imagine, the prison staff were pretty annoyed about that.

So if you are executed in Texas today you must choose something from the standard prison menu. Strange but true - most last meals are cooked by other inmates who work in the prison kitchen. Last meals are usually covered and hidden from other inmates once they are cooked. In the book that follows we will offer an eclectic mix of famous (and not so famous) criminals from history and reveal what they had for their last ever meal. So, make sure you aren't too hungry when you read this book, and prepare to enter the disturbing but darkly fascinating world of killers and food...

BURTON ABBOTT

CRIMES?

Burton Abbott was born in Oregon in 1928. In 1955 he was convicted of the rape and murder of 14-year-old Stephanie Bryan and sentenced to death. Abbott was an accounting student at the University of California at Berkeley around the time when Stephanie went missing. The police were alerted to Abbott when his wife Georgia found items in the house (a purse and some identification) which belonged to Stephanie Bryan. Georgia reported this to the police and Burton Abbott suddenly became the prime suspect in the worrying disappearance of this local girl.

Burton Abbott's mother had actually been the first person to find the missing girl's purse in the house but she had declined to report this discovery to the authorities. She simply refused to believe that her son could have any involvement in this awful case. The senior Mrs Abbott was another in the long line of true crime mothers who refuse to accept that their boy could have done anything wrong.

The most famous example of this phenomenon is Ted Bundy's mother Louise. Louise steadfastly refused to accept that her lovely kind son Ted was a serial killer. "Ted Bundy does not go around killing women and little children!" she told The News Tribune in 1980 after Bundy was convicted for the Florida killings. "And I know this, too, that our never-ending faith in Ted - our faith that he is innocent - has never wavered. And it never will." On his last night alive, Ted Bundy called his mother twice. She told him he was still her son whatever happened.

Burton Abbott's already troubled situation became even more precarious and serious when a pair of spectacles and some underwear belonging to Stephanie Bryan were found in his basement. These discoveries were obviously something of a torpedo hole for Abbott when it came to defending himself. The suspicious connection between Burton Abbott and the missing girl had come to light about three months after her disappearance. The police found Burton Abbott to be unconvincing and shifty when they subjected him to interviews. His evidence often contradicted itself and wasn't very consistent. Abbott appeared to the police to be offering a confusing blizzard of lies in the vague hope that one of them might somehow work and get him off the hook.

Only days later, the body of Stephanie Bryan was found in a shallow grave near Abbott's cabin. After this tragic discovery he was charged with the rape and murder of the girl. The general theory is that Abbott tried to force himself on the girl sexually and, to ensure her silence, ended up killing her when she struggled, cried out, and fought back. Given the decomposition of the body, the pathologist could not officially determine though if a sexual assault had actually taken place.

Despite all the evidence weighted against him, Burton Abbott continued to protest his innocence. As for the items belonging to Stephanie Bryan found in his house, Abbott argued that his house had been used as a polling station in the past so any number of people could have left the victim's possessions there. His protests were to no avail and despite his spirited performance in court he was sentenced to death. On March the 15th, 1957, a one-hour stay of execution from the governor of California was communicated to the prison fractionally too late to halt his execution. By this time, Burton Abbott was already in the gas chamber.

LAST MEAL?

Burton Abbott kept it fairly simple when it came to his last meal - certainly in comparison to the calorie laden junk food binges which would become common sights on death row in the decades to come. He began with French fried butterfly jumbo prawns with cocktail sauce. As we shall see in the book that follows, seafood dishes seem to be quite common when it comes to condemned prisoners facing execution in the United States. Abbott then had some Ravioli. Ravioli, as I'm sure the reader will already know, are a type of pasta comprising a filling enveloped in thin pasta dough and usually served in broth or with a sauce. So it was pasta and fish for Abbott's main courses.

Abbott's main course was very light as far as last meals go as the only other thing he had was a salad in a simple dressing. The salad he ate wasn't very fancy at all and consisted mostly of lettuce. Burton Abbott was clearly a man of simplicity when it came to food. For his dessert, Abbott had some chocolate cake. This was Abbott's one junk food (if chocolate cake qualifies as junk food - you'd probably describe it as a guilty pleasure) indulgence when it came to his final supper. Chocolate cake seems to be quite popular when it comes to last meals on death row. Studies indicate that cake is third after ice cream and pie when it comes to last meal desserts. Abbott also requested and received a pack of Salem cigarettes to enjoy after his meal.

CHARLES ALBANESE

CRIMES?

Charles Albanese was born in Chicago in 1947. He was something of an idle young man but had a stint as a car salesman. Albanese desired most of all to make lots of money without having to work too hard for that money. Join the club Charlie! In that he was a lot like the rest of us. The difference being that Charlie was fully prepared to kill for that money. Most of us want to be rich but we draw the line at actually harming anyone to achieve this. That's the key difference between killers and ordinary people. Killers have a lump of coal where their heart is supposed to be. You could accurately describe Albanese as a financially motivated killer. Radford University's research suggested that 31% of killers murder for financial reasons.

Albanese was another in the long line of true crime poisoners. True crime history is positively (if you'll pardon the pun) laced with murderous poisoners. The victims of Albanese were all relatives of either him or his wife. He killed his wife's mother and grandmother with arsenic in an attempt to shift the family inheritance down a few generations. Charlie would often visit these relatives in a retirement community and bring them gifts and food. They probably thought he was a really nice man. Little did they know he planned to poison them. He was successful in this too and soon had his mother and grandmother in law shuffling off this mortal coil by way of arsenic laced grub.

Charlie's wife (who wasn't part of the poisoning scheme and had no idea her her husband was a murderous criminal) was awarded $150,000 as a result of these murders. The weird thing by this point is that Charlie's father had a Die Casting company and Charles Albanese worked there and earned a decent salary. It isn't as if Charlie was destitute or starved of money. He had a pretty decent standard of living working for his father. Most people would have been perfectly content with the money he earned. It was pure greed which made him also murder relatives for the inheritance. Charlie always wanted more money. They say money is the root of all evil and that was certainly the case with Charles Albanese.

In 1980, the same year as his previous murders, Albanese had a falling out with his father and was demoted in the family company. Charlie seemed to take this demotion surprisingly well though and even began bringing his father cookies as a gift whenever he saw him. No prizes for guessing what was in these biscuits. Charlie's father was poisoned to death by cookies and as a consequence Charles Albanese inherited $250,000 and complete control over the family business. Charlie now had everything he had ever desired. He was awash with money and the family business was his and his alone. What could possibly go wrong? Well, just about everything as it turned out.

The trouble began for Charlie when the McHenry County Coroner, Alvin Querhammer, found arsenic in the body of Charlie's father and so a criminal investigation was launched. The bodies of the two other recently deceased relatives were examined and also found to contain arsenic. The police then discovered that Charles Albanese had been sold some arsenic. The game was nearly up for Charlie. A noose of damning evidence was being drawn ever tighter around his neck.

At this time, Charlie was set to go away with his wife and mother on a trip. The police strongly suspected that Charlie planned to poison his mother on this trip for the last of the family inheritance money. Given what he'd already done, Charles Albanese was probably more than capable of killing his dear old mother. If he had killed his mother then - in terms of statistics - this would have put Albanese in serial killer territory. When the police saw how much money Charles Albanese and his wife had made from the deaths of the three deceased relatives it became rather obvious that he must have been the killer. The evidence against him was overwhelming.

Charles Albanese was tried in two separate jurisdictions and executed via lethal injection at the Stateville Correctional Center in 1995 (as true crime buffs will be well aware, once someone is sentenced to death in the United States it can take years and decades before the execution actually takes place). Albanese never expressed any remorse for his crimes and displayed no emotion in court. He was simply a very cold and ruthless man.

LAST MEAL?

For his last meal, Charles Albanese requested a steak and baked potato. Steaks are very common as a last meal request on death row - which probably isn't surprising. More surprising is the fact that baked potatoes are somewhat popular on death row too it seems - which is slightly strange as you don't tend to think of them as the most exciting food in the world. Would you order a baked potato as part of your last ever meal? I don't think I would.

As a side dish for his steak and potato, Albanese had some garlic bread. Garlic bread consists of bread (usually a baguette or sour dough like a ciabatta), topped with garlic and olive oil or butter and may include additional herbs, such as oregano or chives. Garlic bread is an Italian comfort food. It is often eaten with pasta or pizza.

For his dessert, Charles Albanese had some pistachio ice cream. This was a slightly atypical selection because when it comes to ice cream many death row prisoners go for chocolate or vanilla. Charles Albanese washed his meal down with Coca-Cola (which is VERY popular on death row) and also had a cup of coffee.

STEPHEN ANDERSON

CRIMES?

Stephen Wayne Anderson was born in Utah in 1953. Anderson, a wrong 'un from an early age and always destined for trouble, served some time in prison in the early 1970s for burglary. Most serial killers have criminal convictions from the time before they killed. Sexual offences and robbery are the most common early offences for serial killers. Many serial killers begin their life of crime as thieves and rapists. Anderson inevitably ended up back in prison again - where he killed a fellow inmate in 1977.

While he was prison, Anderson confessed to several previous murders which he seemed to suggest were contract killings. He was sentenced to death but actually escaped and started working as a drug dealer. During these duties he is believed to have murdered again in drug dealing related activity. In 1980, Anderson then robbed the house of 81-year-old Elizabeth Lyman in Bloomington. When she woke up during the robbery he shot her in the face with a handgun. Stephen Wayne Anderson was a vicious man. He had no qualms whatsoever about killing people - however innocent and vulnerable the victims might be.

Anderson's meagre reward for this senseless murder was $100. Anderson, who was clearly no rocket scientist, then continued to loiter in the house of Elizabeth Lyman and even prepared himself some food to eat. Hollywood often depicts serial killers as elusive criminal masterminds who are always two steps ahead of the police. The reality is very different. Many serial killers are of average or below average intelligence and not exactly impossible to catch. Stephen Wayne Anderson was an absolute doddle to catch in the case of this particular murder.

A suspicious and observant neighbour of Elizabeth Lyman (who had obviously noticed that a strange man was wandering around in Elizabeth's house) called the cops and Anderson was swiftly arrested. Anderson was sentenced to death for the second time in 1981 but - as ever - it took many years for the execution to be carried out. On January the 29th, 2002, Anderson was executed by lethal injection at San Quentin State Prison.

The prosecution at the trial had argued that Anderson was so dangerous no one was safe with him INSIDE of prison let alone outside of it. They pointed out that Anderson had once stabbed another inmate while some prisoners were watching a movie together. Stephen Wayne Anderson was one of those criminals who even looked disturbingly evil and crazy in all his mug shots. He definitely isn't someone you would have wanted to meet in real life.

LAST MEAL?

A rather unusual last meal for this ruthless killer. Stephen Wayne Anderson requested two grilled cheese sandwiches. Nothing too strange or unusual about that but he also had some radishes with them. He must be one of the few people in death row history to ask for radishes! Anderson also had a hominy corn mixture. Hominy is made from maize, which is also called field corn. Anderson also asked for some cottage cheese. Not many people would order cottage cheese as their last meal on planet Earth but Anderson did. Cottage cheese is a curdled milk product.

For his dessert, Stephen Wayne Anderson had some peach pie and a pint of chocolate chip ice cream. Peach pie has been popular in Europe and the United States for many years. It is usually served with cream but ice cream is fine too. Anderson's choice of last meal items was somewhat atypical but the choice of chocolate ice cream was certainly very conventional. Who wouldn't want chocolate ice cream as part of their final meal?

Pizza

DENNIS BAGWELL

CRIMES?

Dennis Bagwell was born in 1963. In 1995, Bagwell committed
a brutal spree killing which resulted in the deaths of five
(either blood or step) relatives in Texas. Bagwell was living in a
trailer on the grounds of a rural Texas home where his mother
Leona McBee lived with a man named Ronald Boone. Also in
the house were Boone's daughter Libby Best and his
granddaughters Reba Best and Tassy Boone. Their ages were
24, 4, and 14 respectively. Bagwell, who was in his early
thirties at the time, was living in the trailer with his girlfriend
Victoria Wolford. Bagwell was a petty thief with a cocaine
habit to fund. He would sometimes pawn stuff to buy drugs.

One day, Bagwell said to Wolford he was going into the house
to borrow some money from his mother. His mother hardly
had any money to give him though and this enraged Bagwell.
He shortly went back into his mother's house and Wolford
soon heard screams. Ronald Boone later arrived back at the
house to be greeted by a harrowing scene. Leona McBee and
Tassy had been strangled so violently that their necks were
broken. It was later established that young Tassy had probably
been raped too. Libby had been shot in the head while young
Reba had been bludgeoned to death with a hammer. It was
basically a bloodbath. Dennis Bagwell had gone crazy and
killed a house full of women and kids.

Victoria Wolford later testified against Bagwell. She said that
she'd seen him strike his mother with a gun through the house
window and also heard terrifying screams. She'd also heard
the girls pleading for their lives. You'd imagine that Wolford
had nightmares for life after this tragic and distressing day.
Bagwell then came out of the house and got some water and
cloths in a futile attempt to clean up the blood and DNA
evidence. His plan was to make it look like a home invasion

robbery.

Bagwell's attempts to fool the police didn't get very far at all and this was in no small way thanks to the cooperation of Victoria Wolford. She showed the police the spots where Bagwell had taken evidence from the house and dumped it. The police were also able to extract enough forensic evidence to prove that Bagwell was in the house during the murders. They also matched the spent bullets found in the house to a rifle that he owned. It only took a jury three hours of deliberation to return a guilty verdict and another four hours to sentence Bagwell to death.

Victoria Wolford also told the police that Bagwell was responsible for the murder of 63-year-old George Barry in 1995. George Barry was responsible for making the night deposit in a local bar and Wolford had murdered Barry and then stole two moneybags as a consequence of the killing. Bagwell is believed to have killed Barry by crushing his throat with his boot. Bagwell was convicted of this murder in 1997 and got life added to his slate. Not that it made much difference because he was already on death row for his previous murders. Victoria Wolford got immunity from prosecution as a result of all this information she divulged to the police. On February the 17th, 2005, Dennis Bagwell was executed by lethal injection at the Texas State Penitentiary in Huntsville.

LAST MEAL?

Dennis Bagwell had a generous and uncomplicated last meal. He asked for a steak and some fried chicken. He also had BBQ ribs. Bagwell definitely wasn't a vegetarian, that's for sure. He also had bacon and scrambled eggs with onion. Putting onions or peppers in scrambled eggs is pretty common and gives them a bit of extra zing. That was enough grub to be getting on with but Bagwell wasn't finished yet - not by a long shot. He also had two burgers and some fried potatoes. As a side dish to these courses he had a salad with ranch dressing and some tomatoes. For his dessert, Bagwell had some peach pie. To wash down this last supper, Bagwell had no less than three beverages. He had a glass of milk, iced tea, and - last but not least - a cup of coffee.

VELMA BARFIELD

CRIMES?

Velma Barfield was born in South Carolina in 1932. She had a pretty awful childhood by most accounts and there were stories that her father sexually abused her. At the age of seventeen, Velma got married and eventually had two children. She worked at a factory but didn't last long and was on a battery of prescription drugs. Her marriage was increasingly fractious and in 1969 she took her children and left her husband Thomas Burke. The family home suspiciously burned down at this time - with Thomas Burke (who had passed out) still inside at the time.

Not long afterwards, Velma married a man named Jennings Barfield. Less than a year into the marriage though, Barfield died. The cause of death was believed at the time to be a result of heart problems. He was said to have been having a lot of arguments though with Velma before his swift and unexpected demise. In 1974, Velma's mother died after experiencing severe and painful stomach pains.

Velma was employed as a caretaker around this time but the two couples she was employed to care for also suddenly and mysteriously died. Their symptoms were identical to those of Velma's late mother. You didn't need to be Columbo to suspect that death seemed to follow Velma Barfield around a little too much not to be highly suspicious.

By now, Velma had acquired a boyfriend named Rowland

Stuart Taylor. You can probably guess what happened to him. Before he died, Taylor had deduced that Velma had been forging his cheques. After the death of Rowland Stuart Taylor, the police received a secretive tip that they should investigate Velma Barfield. Taylor's body was exhumed and found to contain arsenic.

When the bodies of others who had died in the proximity of Velma Barfield were examined they were also found to contain arsenic. Velma was arrested and confessed to four murders. She was convicted and sentenced to death - despite objections from psychiatric witnesses who felt she was not of sound mind. Velma Barfield was killed by lethal injection in 1984.

LAST MEAL?

Velma Barfield had one of the more basic and inexpensive last meal requests in the long history of death row. The prison kitchen was not required when it came to Velma's last meal. She simply asked for a bag of Cheez Doodles. Cheez Doodles are a cheese puff produced by Wise Foods. Originally developed and manufactured in 1964 by King Kone Corp. Cheez Doodles are similar to Wotsits or Cheetos. To wash down her Cheez Doodles, Velma had some Coca-Cola. One imagines that the prison authorities would be very happy if all death row prisoners were like Velma Barfield and had a packet of crisps as their last meal. It would probably save them an awful lot of money.

KENNETH BIROS

CRIMES?

Kenneth Biros was born in 1958. In February 1991, Biros murdered 22-year-old Tami Engstrom in Masbury, Ohio. Engstrom was at a bar with with her uncle and had become a trifle drunk. Biros, who evidently knew the uncle, offered to keep an eye on Tami and make sure she was all right. Biros said he'd take Tami out to get some coffee and help her sober up. He promised to fetch her back once she was sober. Tami never went home that night though. The police were notified of her disappearance and given that Biros was the last person to see her that night he obviously became the first person the cops wanted to talk to.

Biros told the police that Tami had got spooked after he touched her leg and that she'd got out of the car and ran across some railway tracks. He said Tammi had hit her head on the tracks and showed the police where the body was. The attempts by Biros to portray this as some sort of accident were not terribly convincing to say the least. When the police examined the body they found some horrendous details. Tammi had 90 knife wounds and her sexual organs had been removed. A breast had been cut off, part of a leg was missing, and her torso had been sliced open. It looked more like the handiwork of Jack the Ripper than a mere accident.

You didn't need to be Sherlock Holmes to deduce that Biros had murdered Tammi and then mutilated the body to satiate some sick sexual fantasy. It was determined by the pathologist that Tammi had been strangled. This was a case of murder - of that there was doubt. At his trial, Brios said that he had chased after Tammi after she fled and then accidentally struck her. He tried to paint this as a case of manslaughter but this defence was not very sturdy at all when subjected to legal scrutiny. Kenneth Biros also denied that he'd had a sexual interest in Tammi during the trial. This was a laughable claim given all the evidence.

Biros was convicted of aggravated murder, attempted rape, aggravated robbery and felonious sexual penetration and sentenced to death. He was finally executed by lethal injection in December, 2009, at the Southern Ohio Correctional Facility in Lucasville, Ohio. Biros was the first prisoner in the United States to be executed with a lethal single-drug dose of the anesthetic sodium thiopental. The US manufacturer Hospira stopped manufacturing the drug in the end and the European Union banned the export of the drug. The reason for this was obviously its use in lethal injections for executions in prisons.

LAST MEAL?

Kenneth Biros kept it fairly simple for his last meal. He had a pizza and as sides he requested onion rings and fried mushrooms. The mushrooms were apparently fried in batter so you could say that he had battered mushrooms. Biros also had some potato chips with a French onion dip. His dessert was slightly atypical because he had cherry pie with blueberry ice cream. Not too many prisoners have gone for this combination. Cherry pie, forever associated with Twin Peaks, was invented in England in 1500 A.D. It is often served with whipped cream. Blueberry ice cream is sort of rare but delicious and has a wonderful blue purple colour. To wash down his final supper, Biros had some Dr Pepper.

OSCAR RAY BOLIN

CRIMES?

Oscar Ray Bolin was born in Indiana in 1962. He had relatives who worked in carnivals and eventually moved to Florida to work in a carnival himself. Bolin was a bit of a drifter - just like this carnival relatives. Bolin's childhood was difficult and unhappy and his parents were not terribly nice to him by all accounts. By the age of fifteen, Bolin was already thieving and getting into trouble with the law. As an adult he would later graduate to rape and murder. In 1982 Bolin was arrested for kidnapping his girlfriend but no charges were filed in the end. He actually married her a year later.

In January 1986, Bolin murdered 25-year-old Natalie Blanche

Holley. Holley was a night manager at a fast food diner in Tampa. After she locked up that night and went to the car park she was never seen again. Her body was found the next day. She was riddled with stab wounds and had clearly been murdered. There was a gap of several months before Bolin murdered again. Near the end of the year 17-year-old Stephanie Collins, a school student, vanished after working a shift at a store. Collins was found exactly a month after her disappearance. She had been stabbed to death. That same day a 26-year-old woman named Teri Lynn Matthews also went missing. She was found hours later with her throat cut. The bodies of the last two victims had been wrapped in blankets and dumped in woodland.

Bolin's spree of terror and murder came to an end in 1987 after he raped a waitress in Toledo with another man. Bolin tried to shoot the victim afterwards but his gun jammed and she escaped. Oscar Ray Bolin was arrested fairly quickly thanks to the traumatised eyewitness. Once he was in custody members of his family began to divulge incriminating details about him to the police. His (now ex) wife told the police that Bolin had confessed to murders and even made her help him hide evidence. Bolin's step-brother said he had seen Bolin beating one of the victims and his cousin said Bolin had raped and murdered 30-year-old Deborah Diane Stowe in Texas in 1987.

Bolin was found guilty and was sentenced to death in July 1991 for the murder of Holley. He was later sentenced to death again for the murder of Collins and received a third death sentence for the murder of Matthews. Oscar Ray Bolin died by lethal injection in 2016. He was never charged with the murder of Deborah Diane Stowe because Texas prosecutors didn't want to complicate and drag out the case too much. The other murders were more than sufficient to get the death penalty.

Before his death, Bolin made headlines in 1996 when he married a woman named Rosalie in prison. This was a case of our old friend hybristophilia. 'Hybristophiliacs,' wrote Owlcation, 'are people who are sexually aroused and attracted to people who have committed cruel, gruesome crimes such as murder and rape. It occurs more often in women than in men. These women are usually delusional and will try to find excuses for what the criminal did. They will develop relationships with a criminal and feel that they are special -- that even though their lover may have killed numerous people, he would never harm her. They usually feel that they can change their lover and have rescue fantasies.'

Hybristophilia is surprisingly common in true crime. Richard Ramirez was said to get plenty of fan mail in prison from women when he was arrested. When he was in prison, Ramirez married magazine editor Doreen Lioy. Lioy had been sending him dozens of letters. Doreen Lioy described Ramirez (who, lest we forget, once plucked out a victim's eyes and put them in a jewelry case for the police to find) as funny and charming. If that's not hybristophilia then nothing is. "I think he's a really great person. He's my best friend; he's my buddy," said Lioy. "I can't help the way the world looks at him. They don't know him the way I do. [People call me crazy] or stupid or lying, and I'm none of those things. I just believe in him completely. In my opinion, there was far more evidence to convict O.J. Simpson, and we all know how that turned out."

Ramirez died of secondary to B-cell lymphoma in 2013 at the age of 53. Doreen Lioy didn't seem to turn up to claim the body of Ramirez when he died in prison. Maybe she was in love with some other evil incarcerated serial killer by this time. In 2009 it had been proven beyond doubt by DNA technology that Richard Ramirez killed a nine year old girl named Mei Leung in 1984. Even the deluded and gullible Doreen Lioy must have felt very stupid and very appalled and disgusted by this scientific cold case revelation. Lioy was not the only person to find Ramirez attractive. Cynthia Haden, one of the jurors at his trial, fell in love with Ramirez and defended him in interviews.

Henry Lee Lucas, Arthur Shawcross, and Randall Woodfield are among the killers who got married in prison. Even Jeffrey Dahmer is said to have got fan mail. You might suggest that Eva Braun, Hitler's mistress and (briefly) wife, suffered from a form of hybristophilia. Afton Burton (aka Star) is the young woman who started contacting Charles Manson in prison and later became engaged to him. She was only 17 when she first contacted him. Burton described Manson as her idol and said she wanted to marry him. He kicked the bucket though before this could happen.

It seems that hybristophilia clouds any sense of logic or taste. Women (and sometimes men) are fascinated by serial killers and even become overwhelmed by the desire to meet them and look after them. They rationalise this conduct by refusing to believe the killer is guilty or simply tell themselves they are doing a kind deed to someone who is lonely and an outcast in society. No matter how awful the killer is, you can guarantee that killer has received fan mail and that there are probably women out there who would be perfectly willing to meet them and, in some cases, even marry them.

LAST MEAL?

For his last meal, Bolin had a rib eye steak and a baked potato. Steak and baked potato seems to be a very popular combo on death row. Bolin had butter and sour cream with his potato. As a side for his meal, Bolin had a simple salad of lettuce, tomato, and cucumber. He also had some garlic bread. Garlic bread also seems to be quite popular on death row too in the United States.

For his dessert, Bolin had some lemon meringue pie. Lemon meringue pie is a type of dessert pie, consisting of a shortened pastry base filled with lemon curd and topped with meringue. This tart sweet and sour dessert is rich and delicious. The origin of this pie is debatable. It has been claimed that a woman in Philadelphia created the lemon meringue pie recipe but meringue fruit desserts existed in France long before that.

It has been alleged too that lemon meringue pie originated in Switzerland. To wash down his food Bolin had some Coca-Cola. The prison officials said that Bolin didn't eat all of his steak and potato but he did finish his portion of pie.

WILLIAM BONIN

CRIMES?

William Bonin was born in Willimantic, Connecticut in 1947. Bonin was known as The Freeway Killer for the way he would pick up hitchhikers and then murder them. Bonin would often dump his victims in some trash after he had killed them. Bonin served in Vietnam as a machine gunner in helicopters. When he left the army though, Bonin slid into a wayward and depraved sort of life. He began to sexually abuse boys and served two prison sentences in the 1970s.

When he got out of prison for the second time in 1979, Bonin decided that the next time he sated his criminal urges to sexually abuse someone they would not live to tell the tale and land him behind bars again. So he began a new career as a serial killer. William Bonin's first victim was a hitchhiker he picked up. The hitchhiker is believed to have been from Germany. Bonin stabbed the hitchhiker over a hundred times and wrapped a nylon cord around his neck. He quickly killed again. There were two more victims in the following days and one of them was only fifteen. The victims were raped and then had their throats slit by Bonin.

Bonin would often prey on homeless men by inviting them home with him. He would frequently prey on victims less able to fight back. His youngest victim was twelve years-old. William Bonin forced one of his victims to drink hydrochloric acid and once used an icepick to stab someone. Bonin once even murdered his best friend simply because his friend was irritating him that day.

William Bonin was one of those serial killers who had accomplices. Vernon Butts and Gregory Miley were young friends of Bonin who knew he was a killer and rapist. Even so, they helped to facilitate his access to victims. Butts and Miley were later arrested and both died behind bars. Bonin's killing spree was ended by a young man named William Pugh. Bonin had given Pugh a lift in his car and then tried to initiate sexual contact. Bonin then told Pugh that he enjoyed killing hitchhikers. Pugh managed to escape from the car because Bonin let him go. The reason Bonin let Pugh go was that the two men had been seen together by other people when they went to Bonin's car. Bonin wasn't stupid enough to murder someone he'd been seen getting into a car with.

The decision not to kill Pugh though would seal Bonin's fate. In 1980, Pugh was in prison for car theft and happened to hear about the exploits of the Freeway Killer on a radio new bulletin. Pugh was pretty sure there was a good chance that this notorious Freeway Killer was William Bonin so he shared his suspicions with the authorities. When the police placed William Bonin under surveillance, they observed him pick up a teenage boy in his van. The officers broke into the van when it stopped and found Bonin sexually assaulting the boy. Scattered around the van were bloodstains, a knife, a nylon cord, and a collection of articles about the Freeway Killer. William Bonin confessed to 21 murders and (after many years on death row) was executed by lethal injection in 1996.

LAST MEAL?

Bonin was clearly a man of simple and predictable tastes when it came to food. Bonin, like most of us, had a weakness for junk food. When the last bell rang on death row for this awful man he requested two pepperoni and sausage pizzas. Pizzas are a very common item when it comes to last meals in American prisons. This is hardly surprising at all as pizza is the ultimate comfort food and something you never get bored of. I think I would find it very difficult NOT to request a pizza if I was granted a last meal.

For his dessert, William Bonin had three bowls of chocolate ice cream. Chocolate ice cream, you won't be surprised to learn, is enduringly popular when it comes to last meals on death row. Bonin washed this repast down with an unholy amount of Coca-Cola and Pepsi. Not the healthiest of meals but then Bonin hardly needed to worry about calories and cholesterol anymore did he? Pizza and chocolate ice cream made a classic comfort food final chowdown for one of the worst criminals imaginable before his impending date with a lethal injection.

ERIC BRANCH

CRIMES?

Eric Branch was convicted and sentenced to death for the 1993 rape and killing of Susan Morris. Susan was a 21-year-old television production student at the University of West Florida. It is believed that Branch initially wanted to steal her car but also ended up raping and killing her. Maybe he planned to do all of these things right from the start. Her naked body was later found in a quiet rural spot. The victim had been violently assaulted before her death. Branch stomped on her face and left a broken stick in her sexual organs. Branch was arrested a few days later in Indiana. The police believe that Branch had spent a couple of days hanging around the Florida campus before the attack. They believe he was searching for a victim.

Branch was no stranger to the criminal justice system. A few years earlier he had been convicted of sexually assaulting a fourteen year-old girl. The great tragedy of the murder of Susan Morris is that it occurred only a few days after Branch had been mistakenly released from a work release correction centre. He shouldn't actually have been able to rape and kill this poor woman because he wasn't supposed to be free at that time. The mistake happened when an employee from the county clerk's office failed to forward a judge's order.

Branch was sentenced to death for this wicked crime and then launched the usual barrage of appeals in an effort to dodge execution. Few people on death row have launched so many appeals as Eric Branch did. He spent over two decades on death row in the end. In one of his appeals he cited this death row confinement as 'cruel and unusual' punishment. He probably should have considered this before he murdered poor Susan Morris. What gave Branch a glimmer of hope in his appeals is that the decision by the jury to sentence him to death had not been completely unanimous (they voted 10 to 2). His legal team doggedly tried to use this detail in the case to their advantage but ultimately all their appeals and arguments were defeated.

Branch had spent 25 years on death row by the time he was executed. Some relatives of the victim Susan Morris attended the execution. They were very calm as they witnessed this moment of closure to a dreadful case. In his last words Branch ranted against his execution and called the prison staff murderers. He screamed a lot when he was strapped to the chair for his lethal injection. This was nothing to do with the execution but simply a case of Branch making a lot of noise in his protests. A lot of death row prisoners are surprisingly calm when the final hour arrives but Eric Branch was not one of these. Branch was a compulsive rapist who is believed to have committed more crimes than exist on official records.

LAST MEAL?

For his last meal, Eric Branch had a T-bone steak and French fries. He had pork chops too so it was a very meat themed last supper. For his dessert, Branch had two pints of Ben and Jerry's ice cream. Steak and ice cream is very typical on death row but Branch was somewhat atypical in his choice of beverage. To wash down this meal he had a bottle of ginger ale. Ginger ale is a carbonated soft drink flavoured with ginger. Ginger ale is believed to have originated in Canada. However, we should probably point out that ginger ale is similar to ginger beer - another ginger themed soft drink which had already been invented in England. Ginger beer is delicious and worth trying if you've never had it before. Ginger beer tends to be punchier and have more of a fiery ginger kick than ginger ale.

Mint Chocolate Chip Ice Cream

ALVIN BRAZIEL

CRIMES?

Alvin Braziel Jr was sentenced to death for a crime he committed in 1993 when he was only eighteen years-old. The crime took place at Eastfield College in Mesquite. Lora and

Douglas White were a young newlywed couple taking a pleasant stroll when Braziel jumped out of nowhere to rob them at gunpoint. Braziel was then enraged when he realised that they didn't have any money. Douglas White was shot dead (he was shot in the head and the heart) while Lora was dragged away and raped at gunpoint. This dreadful incident went unsolved for nearly a decade. In the meantime, Braziel had landed in prison because of a 1995 assault against a teenager.

It was only in 2001 that blood DNA taken from Lora the night of the attack was matched to Alvin Braziel. Lora was then asked to view a police identity parade and picked out Brazier. Her memory hadn't failed her. She still remembered him. As you might imagine, the actual trial was an emotional and difficult ordeal for Lora White because she had to dredge up all the details of what had happened to her and her late husband that night. At one point, she ran from the court in tears when the prosecutor showed her an autopsy photograph of her husband. She said she had not been warned about this and obviously did not welcome this being sprung on her at all. It later transpired though that she had been warned this might happen.

At the trial, Braziel insisted (despite DNA evidence which strongly suggested otherwise) that he was innocent. He even had family members and friends vouch for him and line up to say what a nice man he was. This was all rather dented though by his slate of crimes - which included carjacking, assaults, and high speed car chases. Alvin Braziel was many things but a 'nice man' was not one of those things. Braziel was convicted of capital murder and sentenced to death on July the 26th, 2001.

Brazier's defence team, in their determined efforts to dodge the execution, ventured forth with the familiar litany of (what they argued were) mitigating circumstances. Brazier had a tough childhood, he had a head injury, he was on drugs etc. It was all to no avail in the end though. The police involved in this case believe the only reason Braziel didn't kill Lora White back in 1993 was that his gun jammed. When this happened they think he then decided he would rape her instead.

Braziel was executed by lethal injection on the 11th of December 2018 in Huntsville, Texas. He was 43 years-old. Before he was executed, Braziel offered an apology to the White family though how sincere this apology was is open to question. It is debatable if killers of this type are truly capable of human emotions like remorse and guilt. Lora White eventually managed to start a new life after the terrible ordeal she had been through. She said that, despite all that happened, she prayed for the soul of Alvin Braziel before his death.

LAST MEAL?

Alvin Braziel Jr had a fairly substantial last meal before his execution. He had a pepper steak and steamed rice with brown gravy to begin. Rice and gravy is a staple of Louisiana Creole and Cajun cuisine. Braziel also had ranch style beans. Ranch style beans are tender pinto beans slow cooked in a rich chili sauce. There were pinto beans too as part of this last supper and Braziel had some cornbread to mop up the gravy and beans. Alvin Braziel wasn't full yet because he also had some spaghetti, corn, and garlic toast (garlic bread). Braziel skipped dessert after his meal. Maybe he didn't have much of a sweet tooth? As far as beverages go, Brazier was given some tea, water, and (non alcoholic) punch.

CHRISTOPHER BROOKS

CRIMES?

In 2016, 43 year-old Christopher Eugene Brooks was executed in Alabama for the 1992 murder of 23-year-old Jo Deann Campbell. The murder occurred in upstate New York.

At the time Brooks was working as a counsellor at a summer camp. He was convicted of raping and murdering the victim. Jo Deann Campbell was battered to death with a dumbbell. Her partially clothed dead body was found in her apartment the next day.

Brooks was the last person to be seen with Jo Deann Campbell the night she died and the evidence against him was pretty damning. There would soon be even more damning evidence to come when the forensics team had finished their work. Fingerprints and handprints from Brooks were found both in the apartment and on the body and he was later discovered to also have Jo Deann Campbell's car keys among his private possessions.

When it comes to disposing of bodies, killers vary. Some make an effort to get of evidence and some don't. It really depends on the circumstances of the murder and (in many cases) the intelligence (or indeed mental state) of the killer. A lot of killers leave the victims where they killed them and then flee the scene. There are big differences though in the killers who do this. Richard Chase for example would leave blood all over the place after killing someone. He was quite easy to catch because he left hand and footprints all over his crime scenes.

Danny Rolling on the other hand, while also a gruesome killer, carried cleaning fluids and cloths around with him so that he could clean up his crime scenes and negate the possibility of leaving DNA. Chase was a disorganised killer while Rolling (though equally dangerous) was an organised killer. You would definitely describe Christopher Brooks as a disorganised killer. He left ample forensic evidence and made no attempt to dispose of the body. Brooks was quite easy to catch - which is just as well because he doubtless would have killed again if given the chance.

A jury convicted Christopher Brooks in 1993 of capital murder, robbery, burglary and rape. Christopher Brooks was the first person to be executed in Alabama since the formula of drugs used in the lethal injection had been changed. You could argue then that Brooks was what you might describe as something of a guinea pig in this regard. His legal team fought hard to avoid the execution but it was to no avail in the end. Brooks naturally claimed to be innocent of the murder but there was way too much evidence against him for these protests to have too much in the way of credibility.

LAST MEAL?

Christopher Brooks was cut from the same culinary cloth as Velma Barfield and had one of the simplest and least expensive last meals in the history of American true crime. He simply asked for two Reese's Peanut Butter Cups and a can of Dr Pepper. Reese's Peanut Butter Cups are an American candy consisting of a chocolate cup filled with peanut butter. They are nice but a bit sickly if you eat a few too many of them. If you buy these you should stick them in the fridge because they melt easily.

Dr Pepper is a famous brand of soda pop which is a bit of an acquired taste. It sort of tastes like a mix of cherry cola and marzipan. I'm not a great fan of this stuff myself but it is obviously very popular. Among the flavours in Dr Pepper are alleged to be amaretto, almond, blackberry, black licorice, caramel, carrot, clove, cherry, cola, ginger, juniper, lemon, molasses, nutmeg, orange, prune, plum, pepper, root beer, rum, raspberry, tomato and vanilla. Dr Pepper is quite popular on death row and has been the beverage of choice for a number of condemned prisoners facing execution.

RUSSELL BUCKLEW

CRIMES?

Russell Bucklew was born in 1968. In 1996, in Cape Girardeau

County, Missouri, Bucklew murdered a man named Michael Sanders. Sanders had been sheltering Bucklew's girlfriend Stephanie Ray in his trailer. Stephanie had been subjected to all manner of violent abuse and threats from the jealous and dangerous Bucklew and had finally reached the end of her tether - hence her seeking some shelter and sanctuary with Sanders.

It appears that Bucklew presumed that Stephanie and Michael Sanders were romantically involved and this tilted him over the edge - with tragic and harrowing consequences. Bucklew went to confront Sanders with two handguns. There were kids in the trailer and Sanders, who was armed with a shotgun, got them into a back room before the shoot out began. Sanders fared worse in the duel and was shot twice - one of the bullets from Bucklew's guns hitting him in the lung. He had little chance of surviving.

Bucklew then tried to shoot the six-year son of Sanders but (mercifully) missed. Russell Bucklew then kidnapped Stephanie Ray with handcuffs and drove away from the scene of the carnage. He later raped her in his car. While this was going on Michael Sanders bled to death in the trailer. Bucklew's car details were passed onto the police and he was eventually apprehended - though not before another shoot out in which both Bucklew and a state trooper were wounded.

Bucklew was convicted of first degree murder, kidnapping, and first degree burglary. He received the death sentence. As ever with death row inmates, there were many appeals and legal wrangles. Bucklew's execution finally took place in 2019. Russell Bucklew was an exceptionally dangerous man with a volatile temper. The fact that he owned guns too and was more than prepared to use them meant that some sort of awful tragedy was probably inevitable in the end.

LAST MEAL?

For his last meal, Bucklew requested a smoked brisket

sandwich and French fries. Briskets are the pectoral muscles from the chest of the steer between the forelegs. In this recipe the meat is cooked for a long time so that it almost appears burnt on the outside (though the inside is supposed to be tender and juicy). BBQ is a traditional comfort food in the United States.

Russell Bucklew also had a gyro. A gyro is a food item of Greek origin made from meat cooked on a vertical rotisserie and served wrapped or stuffed in pitta bread, along with ingredients such as tomato, onion, fried potatoes, and tzatziki. A gyro is a kebab really. Bucklew's meal was not exactly sophisticated or healthy but it was rather unusual. It's hard to think of anyone else on death row who went for this particular combination. For his dessert, Bucklew had a banana split (which seems to be quite popular on death row as a dessert). He washed this meal down with some (you guessed it) Coke.

Pecan Pie

JUDY BUENOANO

CRIMES?

Judy Buenoano was born Judias Welty in Quanah, Texas in 1943. Judy Buenoano was known as The Black Widow. She poisoned her husband, drowned her son, and tried to kill her lover with a bomb! Judy, as is so often the case with killers and serial murderers, had a fairly lousy childhood. She was put up for adoption and suffered abuse from both her stepmother and stepfather. At the tender age of fourteen she got a short prison sentence for attacking her step-parents. Judy Buenoano was obviously someone who could only be pushed so far.

Rather than go back to her adopted family (who she clearly despised), Judy chose to go to reform school when her criminal sentence had ended. She left at the age of sixteen and got a job as a nursing assistant in Roswell. She became a mother soon after to a son named Michael Schultz. In 1962 she married an air force officer named James Goodyear and had two more children. She also had a business venture in the form of the Conway Acres Child Care Center in Orlando. James Goodyear died in 1971 of a mysterious illness and Judy cashed in his three life insurance policies. No, nothing suspicious about that at all! She then engineered a house fire to get more insurance money.

Soon after, Judy got a new boyfriend named Bobby Joe Morris. The couple moved to Colorado in 1972 but not before another suspicious house fire occurred. In 1978, Bobby Joe Morris died of a mysterious illness and Judy collected a generous life insurance payout. Judy changed her name to Buenoano (Judy had gone by a battery of various names in the past) around this time and moved back to Pensacola. Judy's son Michael Buenoano had joined the army by this time but he then suffered from very poor health. Michael suffered from paraplegia and wore leg braces. There were signs which suggested someone might be poisoning him.

In 1980, Michael went on a canoe trip with Judy and his brother James. After the canoe got into trouble he was left to fend for himself and ended up drowning because his leg braces were essentially like weights and made him sink. Judy told the authorities it had all been a complete accident and promptly collected Michael's military insurance payout. Judy now opened a beauty salon in Gulf Breeze and began dating a businessman named John Gentry II.

By now though, the authorities were starting to become more than a little suspicious of Judy Buenoano. They found it rather odd that Michael had had three life insurance policies taken out on him shortly before he died. They also found evidence that signatures on these policies might have been forged. Judy Buenoano had told John Gentry a pack of lies about her past. She claimed to be a nurse from Florida. Judy also insisted that they take out life insurance policies on one another.

Another thing that Judy insisted on was that that Gentry should should improve his health by taking some special vitamin tablets she recommended. When these tablets made him feel ill she said he should increase the dose. It was pretty obvious in hindsight that these special tablets of Judy were not vitamin pills at all. In 1983, Judy upped the ante from poisoning and strange canoeing accidents when she put a bomb in Gentry's car!

The police found out that Judy had been going around telling friends that Gentry had a terminal illness and would be dead soon. After a complicated investigation they managed to link Judy to the bomb in Gentry's car. The bodies of Michael Goodyear, James Goodyear, and Bobby Joe Morris were all exhumed and found to contain arsenic. In 1984, Buenoano was convicted for the murder of Michael and the attempted murder of Gentry. In 1985 she was convicted of the murder of James Goodyear. Judy Buenoano went to the electric chair in 1998.

LAST MEAL?

There was no junk food on the menu for Judy Buenoano's last meal request. She kept it simple and very healthy with not a solitary French fry or burger in sight. In fact, you could plausibly argue that Judy Buenoano had the healthiest last meal in death row history. Judy had broccoli and asparagus as her main course - which seemed a rather eccentric selection. I quite like broccoli myself but I definitely wouldn't request it as part of my last meal.

Now, you might presume that Judy would be more extravagant when it came to her dessert. Some ice cream or cheesecake maybe? You'd be wrong in that assumption. Her afters were every bit as frugal as her main course. Judy simply requested some tomatoes and strawberries when it came to pudding. Judy Buenoano's spartan last meal was even evident in her choice of beverage. There was no Pepsi or milkshakes for this condemned death row prisoner. Judy simply asked for a cup of tea. One thing is certain. Judy Buenoano definitely didn't go to the electric chair with indigestion.

TED BUNDY

CRIMES?

Ted Bundy was born in Burlington, Vermont in 1946. Bundy is probably the most famous American serial killer of all time. Ted Bundy is often considered to be the first celebrity serial killer in that he gave television interviews and looked more like a game show host than a deranged killer. Bundy was born Theodore Robert Cowell. He got the name Bundy when his mother married a cook named Johnny Culpepper Bundy. Bundy grew up thinking that his mother was his sister. Ted Bundy's aunt said that, when he was a child, she once awoke to the sight of Bundy carefully placing knives around her sleeping form. Ted Bundy was a peeping Tom as a teenager and also got into trouble for car theft. His elan in stealing cars was something he used to his advantage in his various prison breaks later in life.

Bundy's first official victim was killed in 1974 but he may have killed for the first time in 1961 when he just fourteen. An eight year-old girl named Ann Marie Burr vanished from her Tacoma home in August of that year. At the time, Ted Bundy was the Burr paperboy and lived only four blocks away. Ann Marie's mother later became convinced that Bundy was responsible for her daughter's disappearance but Bundy never confessed to this crime. Bundy was said to have been seen in a construction ditch shortly after Ann Marie disappeared and his uncle was teaching the girl to play piano at the time. All of these details seemed more than mere coincidence.

Ted Bundy was ultimately rejected by his first girlfriend Stephanie Brooks. Bundy said he felt socially out of depth with Brooks. She had brown hair parted in the middle - which obviously led to the theory that Bundy always sought victims who looked like Brooks. Ted Bundy went to the 1968 GOP convention as a delegate for Nelson Rockefeller. It is often suggested that he might have done quite well in politics. What he really wanted to be was a lawyer. He seemed to spend most of his life as a law student although - to his dismay - he was never that smart and found academic life a struggle.

Ted Bundy met a single mother named Elizabeth Kloepfer in 1969 and they had an on/off relationship that ran to 1976. Kloepfer later wrote a book about her life with Bundy. She loved Bundy and wanted to marry him. At first she thought the police suspicion of him was ridiculous but - gradually - she began to have doubts. Ted Bundy was always kind to Elizabeth Kloepfer's daughter. He would sing her lullabies at night. Bundy once worked as the Assistant Director of the Seattle Crime Prevention Advisory Commission. Ted Bundy also worked for the Department of Emergency Services (DES). This was a government agency that searched for missing women.

When he worked for the Seattle Crime Prevention Advisory Commission, Bundy was involved in producing a pamphlet for women on rape prevention.

Bundy would spend a lot of time away from home and it was in 1974 that his activities as a serial killer began to spiral. Bundy would get women into his car by wearing a plaster cast and pretending he needed help carrying some books. One of Ted Bundy's other ruses for getting women into his car was to (with his familiar plaster cast on) pretend he needed help carrying his ski equipment. If you ever wonder where Ted Bundy got all his plaster of Paris from, the answer is simple. He used to work in a medical supply depot. Ted Bundy loved the Volkswagen Beetle. He even stole one of these cars once when he was on the run. The theory is that Bundy liked this car because it was easy to take out the passenger seat and thus easier to get a body into the car and hide it.

Ted Bundy had a custom of killing in the headlights of his car or during a full moon. He liked to see exactly what he was doing. Ted Bundy said that after he killed a woman, he would sometimes shampoo their hair so they had less of an odour. He would have sex with the bodies until decomposition made this impossible. The victims were usually stored in the woods so that Bundy could go back and visit them. Bundy called the part of him that murdered the 'entity'. When Ted Bundy was first at large, the police said they were looking for a man in a Volkswagen Beetle. This didn't really zero the search in on Bundy at first though because the Volkswagen Beetle was a very common and popular car at the time. In order to abduct women from parks, Ted Bundy would wear tennis clothes as if he had just stepped off the court. He would also pretend that he had a sailing boat.

In 1974, a woman named Carol DaRonch had a remarkable escape from Ted Bundy. At the Fashion Place Mall in Salt Lake City, Bundy pretended to be a police detective and told DaRonch her car had been broken into so she she went to the car park with him. Bundy managed to get DaRonch into the car and cuff one of her hands but she managed to get a door open and fight him off. Bundy pulled out a gun but DaRonch - who was obviously terrified - managed to flee. Carol DaRonch later testified against Bundy after his failed attempt to abduct her. People who knew Ted Bundy simply refused to believe he could possibly be a killer at first. These people included the crime writer Ann Rule - who worked with Bundy at a crisis hotline trying to talk people out of suicide. Rule said that Bundy even used to walk her to her car each night after work to make sure she was safe.

Bundy was responsible for the brutal murders of a number of teenagers before the failed abduction of DaRonch. The net was beginning to close though. He was picked out in an identity parade and the police found a ski mask, handcuffs, rope, and a pantyhose mask in his car. Elizabeth Kloepfer, Bundy's girlfriend, had also found plaster of Paris and female clothing in Bundy's possessions. Bundy was charged with the DaRonch kidnap attempt and sentenced to fifteen years in prison. They then managed to connect him to a murder but there was a strange interlude when Bundy jumped out of a window at the Pitkin County Courthouse in Aspen and became a fugitive for several days before being captured again.

Incredibly, Bundy then escaped again by hacksawing through his cell bars and making his way through a crawlspace. He then took the spare clothes of a member of the prison staff and managed to get as far as Chicago. After he escaped from prison, Ted Bundy ended up in Florida where he supported himself by stealing credit cards. He rented a room and pretended his name was Chris Hagen. After he escaped from prison and made his way to Florida, the authorities didn't have the faintest idea where Ted Bundy was. He could have remained undetected for years if his compulsive urge to kill hadn't got the better of him.

In January 1978, Ted Bundy broke into a dorm at Florida State University and attacked four students. One was throttled with a nylon stocking and another was found dead with her nipple bitten off. Another victim had a broken jaw. Bundy left but then attacked a woman several streets away so brutally she was left with a fractured skull. Kathy Kleiner, who survived Ted Bundy's attack on the Florida University Chi Omega sorority house, never went back to the college to finish her studies. When she picked up her stuff from the dorm a week later she noticed there was still blood on the wall. Before his attack on the dorm at Florida University, Ted Bundy hung around the campus and drank in some student bars. He was essentially doing research for his attack and also looking for any stray students he might be able to isolate and abduct.

After the Chi Omega attack, Ted Bundy stole a van and fled. He tried to abduct a 14 year-old girl but her older brother (thankfully) interrupted the abduction and chased Bundy off. Unbelievably, while he was on the road after the Chi Omega attack, Ted Bundy actually met up with a woman for a date. She obviously didn't know he was a serial killer. She thought he was a nice man named Chris Hagen. Ted Bundy's last victim was twelve-year-old Kimberly Leach in 1978. He raped and murdered her in Lake City, Florida. Bundy was not known to target children and it is speculated that Kimberly - tragically - was simply the only victim Bundy could isolate at that time. Ted Bundy's orgy of terror in Florida, and his career as a serial killer, came to an end in the early hours of February 15, 1978. A Pensacola police officer named David Lee noticed the car driven by Ted Bundy suspiciously pull out of an empty car park at one in the morning. Lee verified that the vehicle had been reported stolen and arrested Bundy.

During his last trials, Ted Bundy, acting as his own lawyer, completely shot himself in the foot by asking witnesses too many questions about the specifics of the Florida attacks. This served not only to remind the jury of the awful and graphic nature of the attacks but also made Bundy look creepy because he appeared fascinated by the gruesome details. The conclusive evidence against Ted Bundy for the Florida attacks came from the fact that he had bitten one of the victims on the buttock. Bundy had a chip in one of his teeth that was a perfect match for the bite mark. At his last trial in Orlando, Ted Bundy put his girlfriend Carole Ann Boone on the stand and proposed marriage to her (which she accepted). Carole Ann Boone was a deluded woman who, contrary to all evidence, refused to believe that Bundy was a serial killer. The pair actually had a child together in Bundy's last years. The daughter of Ted Bundy and Carole Ann Boone was the result of a conjugal visit to prison. The prison guards were bribed.

Bundy was fund guilty and sentenced to death. Ted Bundy fought a lengthy battle to avoid the electric chair. This was ironic because his refusal to plead guilty and insistence on defending himself simply made the electric chair more likely. Bundy only became confessional in prison when he sensed that the electric chair was looming on the horizon. He hoped that if he rationed out information about victims and burial places the authorities would decide to keep him alive. It was described as a 'bones for time' strategy. When she found out that her boyfriend Ted Bundy was a serial killer, Elizabeth Kloepfer asked him if he had ever been tempted to kill her. Bundy said that he had thought about it once but would never have gone through with it. In one of his last interviews, Ted Bundy blamed pornography for the dark path his life had taken. It felt like a weak excuse to say the least.

Bundy died in the electric chair in 1989. Ted Bundy's last words before his execution were to pass on his love to friends and family. He was 42 years-old. A large collection of people gathered outside the prison when Ted Bundy was executed. They got drunk and let off fireworks. It turned into a big party. According to one of the guards in prison, Ted Bundy could hear the noise from this party. Ted Bundy's brain was removed after his execution. Medical tests concluded that it showed no sign of abnormality or injury. Bundy requested his ashes be scattered over Washington state's Cascade Mountains. This is where he buried some of his victims.

Bundy is suspected of killing many more people than we can verify. He confessed as much before he died and admitted that he would never confess to all of the killings because they were too 'close' to home. By this he is presumed to have meant that the victims were neighbours or maybe very young. Bundy said that taking a life made him feel like God. He was addicted to the rush and sense of power it gave him. He was truly one of the coldest and most prolific serial killers in American history and all the more chilling because of the charming mask of sanity that he could project to an unsuspecting society.

LAST MEAL?

Ted Bundy declined to specify a last meal and was therefore given a standard generic prison meal of steak, eggs, hash browns, toast with butter and jelly, milk, and juice. He did not eat anything though. Bundy was too scared to eat. He looked apprehensive when he saw the electric chair inside the execution chamber. He seemed to collect himself at this moment though and was then surprisingly calm thereafter.

As for Bundy's taste in food, his former girlfriend Elizabeth Kloepfer said they would often go out for hamburgers. When Bundy was released on bond after his first arrest, he indulged in pizza and beer to celebrate. Bundy was also said to like potato salad. Bundy was actually a decent cook himself and would help out in the kitchen when he visited friends and family for Thanksgiving.

Although he liked simple food like pizza and burgers, Bundy was equally at home if someone took him out for a fancy expensive meal. The real Ted Bundy was a tabula rasa. Bundy was like the lead character in the Woody Allen film Zelig. Zelig tells the story of fictional thirties celebrity Leonard Zelig - a man so insecure he becomes a real life human chameleon who can emulate the speech and appearance of other people when in their company. This was Ted Bundy. He could blend into a university campus, the world of political fundraising, or even a suicide crisis hotline.

Cola

OBA CHANDLER

CRIMES?

Oba Chandler was born in Cincinnati, Ohio, in 1946. He worked as an aluminum-siding contractor but had all manner of criminal misdeeds in his past involving theft, robbery, and peeping Tomdom. Chandler was a bit of a creep to put it mildly. Chandler was convicted for murders which took place in 1989. This incident took place in Tampa and even by the standards of true crime was heartless and distressing.

Joan Rogers and her two daughters Michelle, 17, and Christe, 14, were on vacation in Florida and got lost. They happened to run into Chandler - who offered some directions. It appears that Chandler, who looked harmless enough, had been polite and chatty and invited the family to come out for a cruise of the bay in his boat. Once they were out in the water and out of sight, Chandler tied up the family, weighted them with concrete blocks, and threw them in the water where they all drowned. It is strongly suspected that Chandler sexually abused the woman and two girls before he did this.

What made this crime especially heartless is that the victims were all still alive when they were dumped in the water. Due to decomposition and bloating the bodies floated back to the surface quite quickly but the case went unsolved for nearly three years. A key to cracking the case was identifying the handwriting on a brochure left in the hotel room of the victims. This handwriting was eventually identified as belonging to Oba Chandler. What made Chandler very suspicious in hindsight too was that straight after the murders he had sold his boat and left town.

The police originally believed that more than one person was involved in this awful crime but they eventually decided this wasn't the case. The early suspect was the brother of the father of the murdered girls. This uncle had criminal convictions for rape and was alleged to have had an unhealthy sexual interest in his youngest niece. There was simply no evidence for the theory that he killed his relatives though. Even the grieving husband/father of the victims was a suspect at one point but this was another red herring. Oba Chandler was the killer all along.

Chandler, much to the annoyance of his legal team, admitted to the authorities that he had met the victims but said he only offered them directions and never saw them again after that. Chandler couldn't deny being in Tampa the night of the murders because the police had telephone evidence which showed where his location was that day. Chandler said that he had gone out on his boat that night to do some fishing and was alone. He said he'd called for assistance at one point because his boat broke down. There was no radio evidence though of Chandler calling for any assistance. His evidence was quickly crumbling and falling apart.

Chandler's case became even more hopeless when witnesses

started to come forward. A woman said Chandler had raped her on his boat only weeks before the murders. Friends said that Chandler had bragged about 'dating' three women the night of the murders. Even one of the daughters of Chandler turned against him and said he had implied he had killed people and could never go back to Tampa again. Chandler was found guilty of the murders and sentenced to death in November, 1994. As ever, he then resided on death row for years as legal appeals were filed.

Chandler was finally executed in Florida in 2011. He continued to maintain his innocence right to the end. Some of Chandler's other children also continued to express their belief that he was innocent. Strangely though, Chandler didn't receive a single visitor while he was in prison. Maybe he had instructed his family not to come? In 2014, DNA evidence suggested that Chandler had also been the killer of Ivelisse Berrios-Beguerisse in Florida in 1990. The victim was raped and strangled. It could well be that there are yet more victims of Oba Chandler yet to be discovered.

LAST MEAL?

There wasn't much of a last meal for Oba Chandler on death row and his final supper was indistinguishable from a bog standard prison lunch. He had two salami sandwiches with mustard. He also had a peanut butter and jelly (jam) sandwich. The bread used in these sandwiches was a sliced white loaf.

The first peanut butter and jelly sandwich recipe appeared in the Boston Cooking School Magazine of Culinary Science and Domestic Economics written by Julia Davis in 1901. Peanut butter and jam should not really work as a sandwich but it does. The contrast between the salty peanut butter and the sweet jam is a surprisingly good combination. You need good fresh bread though to make this sandwich really sing. To wash down this modest sandwich meal, Oba Chandler had iced tea and some hot coffee.

RICHARD CHASE

CRIMES?

Richard Chase was born in Santa Clara, California, in 1950. Chase was later nicknamed The Vampire of Sacramento when he achieved infamy as a deranged serial killer. He picked up this grisly and theatrical moniker because he liked to drink the blood of animals and his human victims. Richard Chase was, to put it mildly, messed up from a very young age. He was always tormented by imagined demons and as a child accused his mother of trying to poison him. There was of course no evidence for this - it was merely a paranoid delusion Chase was labouring under. His mother was prone to delusions of her own and was convinced that her husband was secretly plying her with drugs. It was generally an unhappy home to grow up in. There were many arguments and both of Chase's parents were strict and not very affectionate.

Richard Chase had some encounters with juvenile court as a teenager. He is also said to have started taking drugs - including LSD. Biographies of Chase suggest that he was impotent and this apparently caused him great embarrassment and distress - especially when he tried to date some girls. The heavy drug use and delusions of Chase eventually made him impossible for anyone to live with and so as a young man he became dangerously isolated and detached from society.

The fragile mental health of Chase was further illustrated by his preposterous custom of balancing an orange on his head as a way to absorb a daily dose of Vitamin C. One of the most recurring delusions of Chase was the belief that he was the reincarnated spirit of an Old West outlaw. Slowly but surely he was disappearing down the rabbit hole of insanity. Chase was treated at some mental institutions as a young man but in 1976 he was judged safe to be released back into the care of his family and society at large. Hindsight is a wonderful thing but, clearly, this was a huge mistake on the part of the authorities. Richard Chase turned out to be one of the last people in the world you'd want at large in society.

In 1977, Chase was responsible for the murder of a man by means of drive-by shooting. This was a rare case of Chase keeping a victim at arm's length. Chase was soon roaming around neighbourhoods searching for doors that were unlocked. He believed that an unlocked door was a signal to go inside and do whatever he wanted to. At the beginning of 1978, Chase entered the house of a woman who was pregnant and shot her. He indulged in necrophilia with the body and then used a knife to remove some of her internal organs. Chase drank some of the blood of the victim and stuffed dog faeces in her mouth.

Days after this sickening murder, Chase entered another house and shot a man and woman he encountered. He then killed two boys (aged six and two) who were also in the house. Once again, he had sex with the dead female but this time went one step further by eating some of the victim's flesh. As one might imagine, the crime scenes left by Richard Chase were beyond horrific.

Richard Chase was patently not the most careful of serial killers. He seemed to give no thought at all to covering his tracks. Chase was captured very quickly because he left too many handprints and footprints in the blood splatter of the houses he had broken into. When he was arrested, the police found that his vehicle was full of bloodied rags. When the police searched the apartment of Chase they found traces of blood everywhere - including kitchen utensils.

In May, 1980, Richard Chase was convicted on six counts of first degree murder. It is fortunate indeed that he was captured so quickly because the body count would have been considerably higher had he been left to his devices for even a few more weeks. The surprising thing about the Chase trial is that he was judged to be sane and therefore sentenced to death. This man was clearly not sane. Some serial killers often appear alarmingly normal and mundane when they are captured but Chase was not one of them. Gaunt and crazy-eyed with a permanent look of baffled amusement, Richard Chase looked like the complete opposite of sane.

Other prison inmates were said to be scared of Richard Chase because of the insane and brutal nature of his crimes. Even the FBI agents who had to interview Chase were intimidated by him. He projected an oppressive aura of evil indifference and had coal black eyes that seemed to look straight through you. Chase never made his scheduled appointment with the gas chamber in the end. He died in prison in 1980 after an overdose of prescribed antidepressants. The harrowing case of Richard Chase, if nothing else, is a salient reminder of why everyone should always lock their doors at night.

LAST MEAL?

We don't know what the last meal of Richard Chase was but there is a fair chance it might have been cold congealed macaroni cheese. In prison, Chase was still hostage to paranoid delusions and came to believe that the prison staff were trying to poison his food. He therefore took to stuffing his pockets with macaroni cheese as he believed it was the only safe thing to eat. Why he thought the macaroni cheese was safe and everything else was poisoned is anyone's guess.

Trivia - Chase, believing he needed blood to cure his impotence, had a rather strange and bizarre habit of liquidising small animals raw in a blender and then drinking the contents as if it was a protein shake. Richard Chase was so disturbed he even used to inject himself with animal blood.

Fried Shrimp

ANDREI CHIKATILO

CRIMES?

Andrei Chikatilo was born in 1936 in Ukraine (then of course part of the Soviet Union). He would later become known as The Butcher of Rostov and killed over fifty people. Most of his victims were children and he was more than likely responsible for more murders than he was ever convicted of. Chikatilo had a rough childhood and grew up in relative poverty. He is said to have been fascinated by the grisly stories he heard about the war on the Eastern Front (which was naturally right on the doorstep if you lived in Ukraine). The battle between the Red Army and Hitler's Nazi Germany was bestial and ruthless and Chikatilo loved hearing accounts of the mass death, torture, cannibalism, and general misery and carnage that this epic totalitarian conflict had generated.

Chikatilo did his military service and later worked as an engineer. He got married in 1963 but he was said to be impotent (a condition which caused him great distress as a younger man). Nonetheless, the couple had two children - a boy and a girl. Believe it or not, Chikatilo actually became a teacher for a time. He qualified through a correspondence course and became a teacher of Russian language and literature in 1970. This teaching career didn't last very long. There were a series of incidents where Chikatilo was caught trying to fondle or spy on girls in the school and he was dismissed in 1974.

It was from this point that his disturbing career as a serial killer began. Like many serial killers, he targeted vulnerable victims who were less likely to be reported as missing. These were homeless people, drifters, runaways. Chikatilo killed both girls and boys but his preference was for female victims. He sexually abused the bodies after death and would often cut up the bodies with a knife - leaving some gruesome crime scenes. Some of Andrei Chikatilo's victims were missing their uterus and nipples when discovered.

Chikatilo later said that he found he could only satisfy his sexual urges by killing women and children. The act of killing someone and slashing their body up with a knife was very arousing to him. By now a special team of Moscow police had been dispatched to Ukraine to investigate what appeared to be a serial killer. The authorities tried to keep this case out of the media though because, according to communist propaganda, serial killers were supposed to be impossible under the glorious Soviet system. The Soviets liked to pretend that serial killers were the preserve of the wicked and depraved Western nations.

Chikatilo's signature was to remove the eyes of his victims. He said he believed in an old Russian superstition that the imprint of the murderer is left in the eyes of victims. He was constantly on the hunt for fresh victims and always carried a bag around with him that contained rope, vaseline, and a knife. Chikatilo also got into the habit of carrying a towel around with him so that he wipe the blood from his hands.

Chikatilo was arrested in 1984 for sexually assaulting a girl at a train station. The police had no idea he was a serial killer and Chikatilo was released after a year in prison.

Chikatilo got a job in a locomotive factory after his release but his urge to kill got the better of him and he began his murderous exploits again in 1985. Chikatilo killed a dozen or so people in the next five years - many of them children. The police had noticed that many of the victims were found close to railways stations so they planted undercover officers on railways platforms and train workshops. One of these officers observed Chikatilo behaving suspiciously. It transpired that Chikatilo had been on a list of potential suspects since 1987. When the police investigated him further they found they linked him to many of the murder sites.

He was arrested in 1990. Chikatilo seemed rather relieved to have been caught and talked endlessly about his crimes to psychiatrists. Chikatilo's trial was a rather bizarre spectacle. With a shaven head and locked in a cage, Chikatilo frequently shouted over the judge and spouted nonsense. He had been judged sane by the authorities but this man was plainly not sane in the least. He sentenced to death by firing squad and executed in 1994. It is said that he was killed by a single bullet fired behind his ear.

LAST MEAL?

There were no cheeseburgers, French fries, pizzas, or pecan ice cream on offer to condemned men in the Soviet Union. Oh no. Andrei Chikatilo had a very basic last supper of porridge and beef. Beef porridge is actually quite trendy today. This dish is popular in China and is known as congee. The porridge in China has rice. It is probably fair to presume that the dish served to Chikatilo in a Soviet prison wasn't as fancy as the congee you'd get in a modern restaurant.

CARROLL COLE

CRIMES?

Carroll Cole was born in Sioux City, Iowa in 1938. Cole claimed that he killed a boy when he was nine. His father was away during World War 2 and Cole apparently wasn't that close to his mother. As a young man he was in juvenile detention and then joined the US Navy. However, he said he always had a strong urge to kill. Cole would later say that most of his murders occurred after he had got drunk. It probably wasn't a great idea to have a drink with Carroll Cole then.

Cole was booted out of the navy for stealing some guns and spent some time in mental institutions over the next few years. Cole then married (as you do) an alcoholic prostitute. He was soon in prison though for attempting to strangle an eleven year-old girl. When he was released he apparently tried to strangle two women and ended up in a mental hospital. However the doctors there, in a decision that can only be described as insane, decided not to detain him in the end and he was released.

Cole's first murder (if one discounts his claim of killing when he was a child) is believed to have occurred in 1971 in San Diego. Cole strangled a woman in his car and then drove the body around looking for somewhere to dump it. He killed again a few weeks later by strangling a woman and dumping her in the woods. It has been speculated that Cole developed a hatred of women because his mother had a lot of affairs while his father was away taking part in World War 2.

In 1973, Cole got married to a barmaid. You can probably guess how this marriage ended. That's right, Cole murdered her. Believe it or not though, Cole actually escaped charges for her death. The police assumed she must have passed out from drinking and died of natural causes. Cole eventually made his way to Las Vegas where he murdered again. In 1980, Cole strangled three women in Dallas in a single month. By now he must have been starting to lose track of how many people he had killed. They were starting to become a confusing jumble in his mind.

The credited number of victims racked up by Cole though is generally held to be sixteen. Cole was actually found on the scene of the last Dallas murder and arrested. However, in a bungling piece of detective work, the police decided the woman must have died of natural causes and released Cole. At this point though Cole, who was desperate to be caught by now, confessed to this and many other murders. Cole was convicted of three of the murders committed in Texas and sentenced to life in prison. He then had to face the murder charges in Nevada. In October 1984, Cole was sentenced to death in Nevada. He was executed the following year at the age of 47.

LAST MEAL?

There was a seafood theme to Carroll Cole's last meal. A lot of killers on death row seem to crave seafood when the time comes to choose their last ever meal. Cole asked for some Jumbo shrimp to begin. He also requested Boston clam chowder. Clam chowder is a chowder soup which has some regional variations in the United States. It is often thickened with milk and usually served with crackers. Ingredients used in the dish include potatoes, onions, and (you guessed it) clams.

Carroll Cole wasn't finished yet though when it came to his final supper before the date with a lethal injection. He also asked for French fries (French fries seem to be enduringly popular when it comes to Americans prisoners on death row) and also a simple salad with French dressing. Cole's choice of dessert was less elaborate. Cole didn't request a dessert in the end. He simply ate some cookies and chocolate that was left among his prison possessions.

ALTON COLEMAN

CRIMES?

Alton Coleman was a sadistic American rapist, killer, and pedophile. Along with a woman named Debra Denise Brown, he embarked on a harrowing murder spree in 1984 across several states that often targeted children. Women who are accomplices to male serial killers are sometimes able to put together some sort of case for having been forced and coerced into their activities and in some cases were not actually involved in the actual killing. This was certainly not the case with Debra Denise Brown. She participated in the attacks and sexual assaults and later said she had no regrets and had enjoyed them.

The first victim of this awful duo was nine-year-old Vernita Wheat from Kenosha, Wisconsin. Vernita was raped and then strangled. Nine-year-old Annie and seven-year-old Tamika Turks were the next victims. They were both sexually assaulted in brutal fashion. Annie survived (but was left with terrible injuries as a result of the attack - according to a medical report during the trial her intestines were protruding into her lower region as a result of severe cuts) but Tamika was killed.

Coleman and Brown then killed nine-year-old Rachelle Temple in Ohio by strangulation. This evil duo would also often rob people while on the road - often in violent fashion. The next murder victim was a fifteen year-old girl named Tonnie Storey. By now the activities of Coleman and Brown were starting to attract the attention of the FBI and the police and the net was drawing in. The murderous duo stole a car belonging to Harry Walters (the wife of Harry Walters was raped and beaten to death) and then continued to steal cars and assault people. An elderly man named Eugene Scott was later killed in Indianapolis when the duo stole his car.

Coleman and Brown were arrested three days after their last murder. It was decided to put them on trial in Ohio because that represented the best chance of securing the death penalty. Coleman and Brown were both sentenced to death but in 1991 the death sentence for Brown was commuted to life imprisonment by Ohio Governor Richard Celeste. Celeste was a staunch opponent of capital punishment and argued that Brown, who was deemed to suffer from borderline mental retardation, was manipulated by Coleman.

Alton Coleman wasn't so lucky. He was executed in the end - although it took until 2002 for it to happen. There were so many survivors and relatives of victims that his execution was jam packed and didn't have room for everyone. They had to put it on a closed circuit television feed so everyone could witness it.

LAST MEAL?

For his last meal, Alton Coleman went for a very southern theme. He chose filet mignon smothered with mushrooms. Filet mignon is a cut of meat taken from the smaller end of the tenderloin. Coleman also had fried chicken breasts and collard greens. Collard greens are a form of cabbage. They are sometimes called spring greens outside of the United States. Coleman wasn't finished yet when it came to his last supper. He also had cornbread (cornbread is a quick bread made with cornmeal) and a salad with French dressing.

Coleman added onion rings to his meal and also had biscuits and gravy. Biscuits and gravy are tender dough biscuits that are covered in a thick gravy, usually made from the drippings of pork sausages, flour, and milk. Coleman's rather elaborate meal wasn't quite finished yet because he also had broccoli with melted cheese. Oh, I nearly forgot to mention that Coleman had an order of French fries too.

For his dessert, Coleman went for something rather atypical and had sweet potato pie topped with whipped cream. Sweet potato pie is something of an African-American and holiday tradition in the United States. Sweet potato pie is said to taste similar to pumpkin pie. To wash down this generous last feast, Alton Coleman had some Cherry Coke.

Steak and Baked Potato

ROBERT DALE CONKLIN

CRIMES?

Robert Dale Conklin was born in 1961. In March, 1984, Conklin murdered George Crooks - who was his live-in lover - in Georgia. The crime was uncovered when human body parts were found in a trash dumpster outside the apartment block where Conklin and Crooks had lived. There were also knives, a wallet, bloodied linen, a screwdriver, and credit cards (which obviously belonged to Crooks) in the dumpster. Conklin was clearly not the most careful of killers when it came to covering his tracks. It was almost as if he wanted to be caught.

After the grisly dumpster discovery, the police searched Conklin's apartment and found the mattress in the bedroom was splattered with blood stains. The garbage disposal unit in the apartment was clogged with human organs. It was rather like the grisly scene police officers found in the homes of Dahmer and Nilsen. Conklin's guilt was further confirmed when police found a medical book on human dissection in the apartment. This was a pretty open and shut case. Conklin had clearly murdered Crooks and then made a macabre and amateurish attempt to dispose of the remains.

Conklin said to the police that he had wrestled Crooks on the bed and then put a screwdriver in his ear. He confessed to dissecting the body (he could hardly deny that fact given the evidence) and trying to dispose of the remains. Conklin was on parole for armed robbery at the time of the murder. There would be no more parole in his future. In 2005, the 43 year-old Conklin was executed by lethal injection by the State of Georgia.

LAST MEAL?

Conklin, as far as killers go, was a man of quite refined tastes when it came to grub. There were no cheeseburgers, French fries, or pizzas for this condemned man. He had filet mignon wrapped with bacon and some shrimp in garlic butter with lemon. Conklin also requested asparagus with hollandaise sauce. Hollandaise sauce, formerly also called Dutch sauce, is a mixture of egg yolk, melted butter, and lemon juice. It is usually seasoned with salt, and either white pepper or cayenne pepper. As a side dish, Conklin had a baked potato with sour cream, chives and bacon bits. Conklin was yet another death row prisoner with a weakness for the humble baked potato.

Conklin wasn't finished yet when it came to his main course because he also asked for some corn on the cob and goat cheese. Goat cheese is a bit like feta and has a mild creamy sort of taste and texture. For his dessert, Conklin asked for vanilla ice cream, apple pie, and some cantaloupe. Cantaloupe is a type of melon. There was no Pepsi or Coke for Conklin with his last meal. He washed this somewhat elegant final supper down with iced tea. Iced tea, as the name implies, is tea served cold with ice. It is a refreshing drink in summer months.

JOHN WAYNE CONNER

CRIMES?

In 2016, 60 year-old John Wayne Conner was executed by lethal injection by the Georgia Department of Corrections for a murder he committed in 1982. Conner beat his friend J.T. White to death. It was a dreadful attack. After a night of drink and drugs, Conner turned on his friend and viciously beat him with a spirits bottle and piece of wood. Conner claimed that White had enraged him because he articulated a sexual interest in Conner's girlfriend. A fight ensued - which soon became tragically serious.

White's body was later found hidden in a drain ditch. Conner had tried to hide in a barn (his plan was to lie low and then flee with his girlfriend but this plan obviously didn't get very far at all) after the murder but he was quickly found by the police and taken into custody. He was 25 years-old at the time of the murder.

Conner spent three long decades on death row for this murder. His legal mounted a spirited and prolonged defence against the death penalty but it was ultimately to no avail. They had argued that Conner grew up in an abusive home where drugs and violence were rife. They also argued that Conner suffered from a mental impairment and so was not competent enough to be punished through a formal trial (as he obviously had been).

His lawyers argued that while this did not mitigate his

dreadful crime it would be sufficient enough punishment for him to spend his life behind bars and an execution was not necessary. They were ultimately unsuccessful in this argument. John Wayne Conner made no final statement before his execution and declined the custom of having a prayer said for him.

LAST MEAL?

Though uninterested in statements and prayers, John Wayne Conner made the most of the last meal custom and requested a generous final supper. He ordered ten hushpuppies to begin. A hush puppy (or hushpuppy) is a small, savory, deep-fried round ball made from cornmeal-based batter. Hushpuppies are frequently served as a side dish with seafood and other deep-fried foods. Conner also had ten pieces of fried catfish - which is a classic southern fast food dish. John Wayne Conner was yet another death row inmate partial to a bit of seafood.

Conner also asked for two triple hamburgers with bacon. His last food request was a sliced onion. Whether this for the burger or fish is unknown. Maybe it was both? Despite this hearty meal, Conner still had room for afters and finished off with two pints of vanilla ice cream. How much of this meal John Wayne Conner managed to eat is not known. His last meal request sounded rather like a Man vs Food challenge.

RICHARD COOEY

CRIMES?

Richard Cooey was born in Akron, Ohio in 1967. In 1986, the then nineteen year-old Cooey was on leave from the army and with two friends throwing rocks onto cars racing along a highway below. As you might already have gathered, Cooey was a stupid and odious young man. Dropping rocks onto cars was a very weird and dangerous thing to do but that wasn't the worst of it. Not by a long shot.

Two cars eventually had to stop because of damage from the falling rocks and the drivers were 21-year-old Wendy Offredo and 20-year-old Dawn McCreery. Cooey and his friends pretended to be offering aid and assistance but then, after dragging the victims away to a secluded spot, raped, tortured and killed the two woman. The two women were beaten to death and mutilated. Cooey's chief assistant (Kenneth Horonetz) in these crimes was too young to get the death sentence so got life in prison. Cooey had no such luck. He DID get sentenced on death.

The two woman were choked and bludgeoned to death and had an X carved on their stomachs. Cooey and Kenneth Horonetz (predictably) tried to blame one another for the murders. They were both vile men but Cooey was seen as the main instigator and most active in the murders. One of Cooey's friends had fled before the violence began. It was cowardly and wrong of him not to stay and protect the women but at least he hadn't been involved in their rapes and deaths. Cooey was stupid enough to brag about the murders to friends and in the end one of them turned him in to the police.

Richard Cooey then claimed that he'd raped the women but did not kill them. No one believed this was true though. He said he was drunk and high at the time of the incident - which was certainly a lot easier to believe. Cooey was finally executed by lethal injection in 2005. The year before he had unsuccessfully tried to escape from prison. Cooey and his legal team had argued that because of his huge weight he should not be killed by lethal injection because it would difficult and painful to find a vein. Theses objections were all rejected though and the execution went ahead as planned.

LAST MEAL?

Cooey, as one might expect of a 275 pound man, ordered a

hearty last meal. He had T-bone steak, onion rings, French fries, fried eggs, hash browns, and toast. It was what you might describe as a classic diner blowout. Hash browns consist of finely chopped potatoes that have been fried until browned. Onion rings are a classic comfort food. An onion ring consists of a cross-sectional ring of onion dipped in batter or bread crumbs and then deep fried.

For dessert, Cooey asked for rocky road ice cream. Rocky road ice cream is a chocolate flavoured ice cream which usually has marshmallows. Cooey wasn't finished yet though when it came to his final supper. He also had some room for bear claw pastries. A bear claw is a sweet, yeast-raised pastry, a type of Danish. Cooey washed this feast down with Mountain Dew. His stomach full, he retired for the night as the last hours and minutes to his death by lethal injection continued to tick away.

JEFFREY DAHMER

CRIMES?

Jeffrey Dahmer was born in Milwaukee in 1960. Relatives of Jeffrey Dahmer say that his personality seemed to suddenly change after he had hernia surgery at the age of six. Dahmer became very interested in taxidermy and decomposition. Jeffrey Dahmer's chemist father taught him how to preserve animal bones. He was a very bright kid and had an IQ of 145 as an adult. However, he developed a drinking problem at a young age - which seemed to blight whatever potential he had. Dahmer was also gay and so all of his future victims would be men that he had picked up or developed a friendship with.

When he was growing-up, Jeffrey Dahmer once stole a mannequin from a store and kept it in his bedroom. He had a sexual fantasy where he dominated an inert lover. This fantasy was by no means uncommon when it came to serial killers.

Dahmer said he first had a fantasy about killing someone when he was in high school. He is believed to have killed for the first time when he was eighteen. Dahmer murdered a hitchhiker he had picked up by hitting him with a weight. Dahmer used acid to dissolve the body and crushed whatever bones were left with a hammer.

After dropping out of university, Dahmer became a combat medic in the 8th Infantry Division and was stationed in West Germany. Two soldiers who served with Dahmer claimed that he sedated and raped them in Germany. Jeffrey Dahmer was eventually kicked out of the army for his drinking though. After he was discharged, Dahmer went home and worked in a chocolate factory before moving in with his grandmother. Dahmer began to pick up men and there were more incidents of him sedating and sexually assaulting victims. In 1987, Jeffrey Dahmer woke up in a motel with the dead body of a man next to him. He somehow managed to get the body out of the motel using a suitcase and took it to his grandmother's home (where Dahmer lived) so that he could dissect the body and dispose of it.

Soon after, Dahmer moved into an apartment and his killing spree began to spiral out of control. Jeffrey Dahmer said he tried to stop killing but it was a compulsion he just couldn't ignore. Jeffrey Dahmer's apartment was so eventually so full with victims and body parts that he put one body in the bath and had to shower over it. The apartment contained a plastic drum of acid where three human torsos were dissolving. Jeffrey Dahmer poured acid into the head of a victim named Konerak Sinthasomphone. Sinthasomphone escaped and wandered the streets in a daze. Tragically, some policemen who found Sinthasomphone then took him back to Dahmer's apartment after Dahmer told them Sinthasomphone was his intoxicated boyfriend. Dahmer was so crazy that he thought if he injected acid into a victim they would become a complient slave for him.

Dahmer would sedate his victims by giving them a drink that

was laced with sleeping pills. Dahmer once drank the spiked drink he had laced for a victim by mistake. He passed out and when he woke up the victim had robbed him and left. Naturally, Dahmer didn't bother to report the crime. The 'thief' had no idea how lucky he had been that Dahmer gave him the wrong drink by mistake. Dahmer is most famous for the fact that he would eat parts of his victims. Jeffrey Dahmer fried the body parts of his victims in a skillet before he ate them. Dahmer used a meat tenderizer to make human flesh more edible.

Dahmer liked to paint human skulls because he thought this made them look fake and they would be less suspicious if discovered. He used formaldehyde to preserve body parts. Jeffrey Dahmer was captured when a man named Tracy Edwards managed to escape the handcuffs Dahmer had put on him and go and fetch some police officers. Dahmer had two hands and human genitalia in his kettle when the police searched his apartment. This was merely the tip of the iceberg. One of the police officers later described Dahmer's apartment as like entering a real life horror museum. It was very grim and disturbing.

The police found a complete skeleton in Jeffry Dahmer's filing cabinet and three human heads in the fridge. Dahmer seemed relieved to have been caught and spent hours giving them a full confession. In his confession, Jeffrey Dahmer said that when he cut up his victims he would remove his clothes and place the victim in a tub. He said he felt brief remorse for the victim but this did not last. Mostly, he felt excited. When he was captured, Jeffrey Dahmer told the police that he retained the skulls and bones of his victims because he wanted to use them to construct a place of meditation.

Dahmer said that, circa 1983, he tried to use religion to fight off his desperate urge to kill. It obviously didn't work. Dahmer was tried in Milwaukee for 15 counts of first-degree murder. The death penalty was not an option in the state so Dahmer was sentenced to life behind bars. He did some interviews while in prison. Despite the gruesome and unfathomable nature of his crimes, Dahmer seemed alarmingly normal and mundane in interviews. He was articulate and soft-spoken. Dahmer didn't serve much of his sentence in the end.

In 1994, another prisoner (a convicted murderer named Christopher Scarver) attacked Dahmer and another inmate named Jesse Anderson with an iron bar after some sort of altercation. The attack was so violent that Dahmer later died in hospital. He was 34 years-old and the life of one of the most infamous serial killers in American history had ended.

LAST MEAL?

The last thing ever eaten by Dahmer before he was killed in prison was a toasted cheese sandwich. This was a very run of the mill last meal for one of history's most notorious cannibals.

During his police confession, Jeffrey Dahmer was asked if he ate human body parts plain. He replied that he ate them with salt & pepper and steak sauce. Neigbours of Jeffrey Dahmer did complain about the smell coming from his apartment once. He apparently told them that his fridge broke and some food went bad. Dahmer had a tray at the bottom of his fridge to collect the blood that dripped down from body parts.

Jeffrey Dahmer would sometimes make sandwiches for neighbours in his apartment building. It is therefore possible that his neighbours might have unwittingly eaten human flesh.

Want some trivia that will never be of any use to you? When the police searched Jeffrey Dahmer's apartment he had VHS tapes of Return of the Jedi, The Exorcist II, Chippendales Tall Dark and Handsome, and an episode of The Cosby Show.

ALAN LEE DAVIS

CRIMES?

Allen Lee Davis was born in Florida in 1944. Like many killers, Davis was a habitual criminal from a young age and involved in violent robberies. He is also said to have been a child abuser. In May 1982, Davis beat Nancy Weiler to death in her Florida home and then shot dead her two young daughters. Weiler was pregnant at the time of her death - adding another layer of tragedy into a case that was already unspeakably sad and awful. It is beyond comprehension that anyone would be capable of shooting an innocent child but - sadly - it does happen.

Davis was on parole for armed robbery at the time of this indescribably terrible attack. He said that his motive had been to rape Nancy Weiler and then rob the house but things began to spiral out of control and there were more people in the house than he expected. David was one of those people who just LOOKED evil. He had blank dark eyes and an expressionless face. He was sentenced to death and finally executed by way of the electric chair in 1999.

The execution of Allen Lee Davis provoked controversy because photographs were later released of him in the electric chair with blood pouring from his facc. Thc official verdict of the authorities after an investigation was that nothing went wrong with the electric hair and the blood was a result of medication Davis was on. This verdict felt less than convincing and certainly created some debate about the death penalty.

Should a civilised modern society really still be killing criminals with an electric chair in 1999? No one would dispute that Davis was an evil and vile man but it was a distressing and worrying incident all the same. It is worth noting that since the execution of Allen Lee Davis no other prisoner has been killed in Florida by the electric chair. This would appear to be some sort of tacit admission that something did indeed go wrong when Davis was executed.

LAST MEAL?

Allen Lee Davis, like so many death row inmates, was clearly a fan of seafood. For his last meal he had a mountain of shrimp and clams - all of it fried. He also had a lobster tail. The lobster was the one touch of luxury in the meal requested by Davis as most of it was fairly simple down to earth grub. Davis wasn't finished yet. As a side dish he had potatoes and garlic bread. This was all washed down with root beer. Davis was slightly unusual when it came to last meals in that he seems to be one of the few prisoners who decided to skip dessert. Maybe he was too full up after his main course.

Fried Chicken

WESTLEY ALLAN DODD

CRIMES?

Westley Allan Dodd was born in Toppenish, Washington, on July 3, 1961. Dodd was a strange boy who the other kids tended to shun. In his early teenage years he developed a propensity for indecent exposure - which earned at least one arrest. Dodd had also started to molest children, something that his occasional babysitting duties facilitated. Although he once tried to abduct two little girls, Dodd's sexual preference was young boys.

In the early eighties he joined the Navy but he still couldn't stay out of trouble. He paid two boys $50 to play strip poker and was arrested - although, strangely, no charges were brought against him. In 1984 he was arrested again for molesting a young boy but received only a suspended sentence. The warning signs were more than apparent but the authorities never seemed to take any firm action against him. Dodd was discharged from the Navy and became a somewhat nomadic figure, moving around and taking various jobs. He chose occupations and apartments that would give him ample access to children.

There were further molestation incidents and in 1987 Dodd tried to lure a young boy into an abandoned building. He was placed on probation though rather than given a prison sentence. This was a mistake that would have tragic consequences. Dodd was a grave danger to children and should not have been left to his own devices. Dodd moved to Vancouver and soon deduced that David Douglas Park was both secluded and popular with children. He is said to have molested up to fifty children thereafter but only received short prison sentences for his crimes.

In 1989, Dodd targeted two brothers - 11 and 10 year-old Cole

and William Neer - in the park. He tied them to a tree,
molested them, and then stabbed them. They both died of
their injuries. On October 29, Dodd drove to Portland, Oregon
and there he encountered four-year-old Lee Iseli and his nine-
year-old brother Justin at a local park. Dodd managed to
isolate Lee and took him home to his apartment. He tied the
boy to a bed, molested him, and then strangled him to death
the next morning with rope. By now, Dodd had taken to
writing a diary detailing his murders. He also took pictures of
his victims. He was a disturbed and dangerous man.

Dodd's awful activities came to an end when he tried abduct a
6-year-old boy from the restroom of the New Liberty Theater
in Camas, Washington. When the boy struggled, cinema staff
intervened and Dodd fled in his car. The boyfriend of the boy's
mother arrived on the scene and noticed that Dodd's car had
broken down just down the street. He managed to detain Dodd
in a headlock and the police were called. Under police
questioning, Dodd eventually confessed to the murders he was
responsible for.

When they searched Dodd's house, the police found a torture
rack, his diary (with details of his crimes), the underwear of
one victim, and various photographs of children. Dodd was
charged with first-degree murder in the deaths of the Neer
brothers and Lee Iseli, plus attempted kidnapping of another
child. Despite his earlier confession, he initially pleaded not
guilty to all charges but then later changed his plea to guilty.

In 1990, Dodd was sentenced to death for the murder of the
Neer brothers, as well as for the separate rape and murder of
Lee Iseli. Dodd, under Washington state law, was given the
choice of hanging or lethal injection. He chose hanging as he
felt it was appropriate that he be killed by rope as he had
murdered one of his victims by this method. Dodd was
executed by hanging at 12:05 a.m. on January the 5th, 1993 at
Washington State Penitentiary in Walla Walla.

LAST MEAL?

For his last meal in this mortal realm, Westley Allan Dodd (who was YET another death row seafood fan) ordered broiled salmon and potatoes. Dodd's last meal must rank as one of the healthiest any condemned prisoner has ever chosen! They usually go for burgers or pizzas and ice cream. Salmon and potatoes is what you could describe as good rustic food. Baby potatoes are often used in this famous food combination.

ALBERT FISH

CRIMES?

Albert Fish was born in Washington, D.C. in 1870. If every age has its own bogeyman then it can be said that Albert Fish took on this role in the early decades of the 20th century. He molested over 400 children and tortured and killed others. We will never know exactly how many people Fish might have killed. Albert Fish said his greatest pleasure in life was to inflict pain. Fish grew-up in an orphanage and the regular beatings the children received there seemed to activate a sadomasochistic enjoyment of pain (both giving and receiving) in Fish. Fish liked to be hit with a spiked cane as an adult. As a boy he was a Peeping Tom and when he began experimenting with homosexual relationships he discovered that he enjoyed watersports. And no, I don't mean water skiing.

One of the strangest things about the disturbing life of Albert Fish is that he got married and had six children. This marriage was arranged by his mother but Fish was said to be a good father - despite the fact that in his private life he was out raping boys. He landed in prison a few times for theft but his more serious crimes seemed to evade the notice of the authorities - for a time at least. Fish moved from New York to Wilmington around this time. His occupation was a house painter and this often meant he had to travel to get some work. In Wilmington he began a secret relationship with a teenager named Thomas Keddon. Fish cut off the genitals of Keddon and left him bleeding and tied up in a farmhouse. No one is sure what happened to Keddon in the end.

Fish claimed that he killed and raped other children in the period that followed. There was an incident where he stabbed a mentally handicapped boy and he killed a child named Francis McDonnell. The flesh from one of the child's legs had been hacked away. Fish always claimed to be a cannibal. He once told the police that he made a stew out of the nose and ears of one of his victims. No wonder Albert Fish is considered to have been one of the inspirations for Hannibal Lecter.

The most infamous crime of Fish came when he pretended to be hiring farm workers and met the Budd family (whose father Edward was seeking employment). Fish persuaded them to let their ten year-old daughter Grace visit him to attend a birthday party for his niece but - of course - it was all a ruse and Grace turned up to find Fish alone. Fish later sent the Budd family a letter in which he claimed to have cooked and eaten Grace after he killed her.

The awful mocking letter that Albert Fish wrote to the Budd family sealed his fate. The authorities were able to deduce that Fish used stationary from the New York Private Chauffeur's Benevolent Association (Fish was actually working as a chauffeur at the time) and managed to find out where he was living. Fish died in the electric chair in 1936. He seemed to welcome the chance to sample the electric chair. Fish said it would be a great thrill. X-rays taken of Fish when he was in custody revealed twenty needles he had pushed into his groin. He was a seriously strange and disturbing man.

LAST MEAL?

The last meal of Albert Fish was a bit strange because he was afforded a final meal before execution but then the execution was delayed so Fish ate the food with his family. And what did Fish order for his last supper? Well, he requested dried fish and sardines. That must surely rank as one the least appealing last meals ever requested in the history of crime! Maybe he just loved eating seafood?

Albert Fish was of course executed (for good) at a later date but we don't know if he was afforded a second last meal this time. If he was was he doubtless asked for some fish again if his first 'last' meal was anything to go by. We can safely say that very few people in the world would willingly choose dried fish and sardines as their last meal.

EARL FORREST

CRIMES?

Earl Forrest was born in 1949. His crimes took place in Missouri. Forrest was a drug dealer who originally operated in California. He had a good life with lots of money but moved to Missouri because he feared he was becoming a little too well known to law enforcement agents in California. In December, 2002, Forrest went to the home of Harriet Smith for what was supposed to be a business transaction. It was a pretty weird and illegal transaction to say the least.

Apparently, Forrest had arranged a deal with Smith where she would procure him a lawn mower in return for him supplying her with a way to get methamphetamine. Methamphetamine is better known as crystal meth. As we shall see, that elusive lawn mower would - bizarrely - play a crucial role in this dreadful case. It would probably be the understatement of the century to say that this unusual business transaction didn't quite go according to plan. At some point tempers got frayed. It appears that Forrest felt that Smith was attempting to renege on her part of the bargain. Given her reliance on crystal meth she probably wasn't the most reliable person in the world to do business with. That hardly justified what happened next though.

A friend of Smith named Michael Wells, unfortunately for him, was also present. Forrest shot Wells in the face and then shot Harriet Smith six times. Forrest then took all the drugs he could find and went home - where the police soon cottoned onto him. A shoot out took place and Forrest shot and killed Deputy JoAnn Barnes. Forrest actually knew JoAnn Barnes because she had arrested him once for a parole violation. He then shot his girlfriend and another police officer (Sheriff Bob Wofford) but thankfully these two survived. You probably won't be surprised to hear that Earl Forrest had been drinking heavily on this tragic day. He was crazy, angry, drunk, and highly dangerous. He also got high on meth before he shot at the police officers.

Forrest's crimes were about as serious as it got. He was facing a likely death sentence anyway for the two initial murders but then he made it even worse (if it could actually get any worse) by shooting dead a police officer. Forrest, in what was no surprise, was sentenced to death at his trial. His legal team used a familiar defence and said that it should be taken into account that Forrest had a bad brain injury which affected his behaviour. They actually had medical proof of this too from a scan. They wanted Forrest to be spared execution and just spend his life behind bars but these arguments were thrown out in the end.

In 2016, Earl Forrest was put to death by lethal injection at the Eastern Reception, Diagnostic and Correctional Center in Bonne Terre. Forrest gave a television interview shortly before his death. He was surprisingly articulate and calm given his case file. Forrest said that he'd killed Smith because she didn't buy him a lawn mower as promised. Forrest said his ex-wife had sold his old lawn mower and he had a big lawn. He said he'd felt that Smith had taken him for a 'punk' and soft-touch and he wasn't going to stand for that. Forrest said that he'd liked Michael Wells and had some remorse about shooting him. He said he had no remorse though about shooting Smith and Deputy JoAnn Barnes. Perhaps the only lesson we can glean from this awful case is this: if you ever promise to buy someone a lawn mower make sure you actually deliver it as agreed!

LAST MEAL?

For his last meal, Earl Forrest had a steak and some pasta. He also had sliced tomatoes and cucumber. Forrest asked for a fruit plate with his meal. A fruit platter if you prefer. As the name implies, different fruits on a plate. It was a surprisingly healthy main course for a former drug dealer. For his pudding, Forrest had some chocolate cake. Earl Forrest evidently wasn't a soda person because his last supper beverage of choice was milk.

Cheez Doodles

JOHN WAYNE GACY

CRIMES?

John Wayne Gacy was born in Chicago in 1942. Gacy is one of
the most evil serial killers in the history of the United States
and given the competition that's really saying something. Gacy
worked as a mortician's assistant as a very young man and
later seemed to confess that he had once fondled one of the
corpses there. Although he had a wife and family, John Wayne
Gacy was secretly gay. His family man image was useful
though as a sort of disguise. When he got married, Gacy
worked for a shoe company and was involved in The United
States Junior Chamber (the Jaycees). This was a leadership
training and civic organisation for people between the ages of
18 and 40. As a young man, Gacy had worked as assistant
precinct captain for a Democratic Party candidate in his
neighborhood. He was once even introduced to the First Lady
Rosalynn Carter at a function for the Democratic Party.

Gacy changed occupations when he became the manager of a
Kentucky Fried Chicken franchise. Gacy's secret life was dark
and disturbing. In the late 1960s, Gacy sexually assaulted a
fifteen year-old boy named Donald Vorhees. Gacy then gave
another boy some money to beat up Vorhees so that he would
be too intimidated to testify in a court. Gacy had sexual
relations with many teenagers and boys and he didn't really
care about the age of consent. Donald Vorhees refused to be
intimidated though and told the police about Gacy. Gacy was
sentenced to ten years in prison for underage sexual assault
but he was such a model prisoner he was out on parole after a
couple of years. He lived with his mother for a while and then
got engaged so that he could have have a new family.

This new relationship gave Gacy two stepdaughters. Gacy
started a construction business and purchased a house in
Norwood Park Township, an unincorporated area of Cook

County. The construction business was a big success and made Gacy financially secure. Once again, Gacy was playing a role he loved - that of the solid citizen and pillar of the community. He was even dressing up as a clown to entertain the local children.

Gacy murdered 33 teenage boys and young men between 1972 and 1978. John Wayne Gacy's access to victims was provided by his construction business. He was constantly in contact with teenagers and young men looking for some temporary work. One of John Wayne Gacy's methods in getting his victims handcuffed was to pretend he was demonstrating a magic trick. He would escape from the handcuffs himself and then challenge the victim to do the same. Gacy would usually try and get his victims a bit drunk for this game. By the time they realised it was not a game and that Gacy was dangerous it was all too late. They were already helpless. John Wayne Gacy weighed 230 pounds. He was a big man who would have been difficult to fight off - especially if one was restrained.

John Wayne Gacy stuffed the bodies of most of his victims in the crawlspace of his home. When his wife asked about the smell he told her it was mice. Gacy used his experience as a mortician's assistant to block the cavities of his victims with rags and underwear. This prevented too much leakage after death. John Wayne Gacy would sometimes contact the police and report one of the men he had killed as missing. This was a tactic designed to make him seem trustworthy and throw the police off his scent. When his crawlspace started to get too full up with bodies, he used his car to throw dead victims off the I-55 bridge into the Des Plaines River.

A teenager named Robert Priest was then reported missing and the police, upon further investigation, deduced that one of the last things Priest had done before he vanished was to visit John Wayne Gacy to talk about a job. The police, investigating Gacy further, now discovered the sexual assault conviction that had landed him in prison years ago. Further evidence against Gacy came from a young man named Jeffrey Rignal. The police learned that Rignal had accused Gacy of drugging and raping him.

When the police obtained the legal right to search the house the game was finally up for Gacy. The crawlspace in his house was one of the most disturbing sights these detectives were ever likely to witness. Some of the bodies had become fused together in decomposition. Many of John Wayne Gacy's victims were found to have rope tied around their neck.

It was an exceptionally complex and time consuming task to identify all of the victims. Sadly, to this day, there are still victims of Gacy yet to be identified. Gacy was killed by lethal injection in May, 1994.

LAST MEAL?

Gacy was allowed to have a last picnic with his family before his execution. For his last meal Gacy requested 12 fried shrimp, a bucket of original recipe KFC, French fries, and strawberries. As for 'original' recipe KFC (KFC was not a term when Gacy worked for them - it had yet to be rebranded), it could be that Gacy wanted the old Kentucky Fried Chicken from when it was fried in vegetable oil. By the time of Gacy's execution, many branches of KFC had switched to using different sorts of oil. The actual KFC recipe (which is allegedly locked in a vault) hasn't changed over the years.

Trivia - Gacy is said to have done 2,000 paintings while he was on death row. The Tatou Art Gallery in Beverly Hills tried to sell some of John Wayne Gacy's paintings. They were described as art brut. Legend has it that Johnny Depp owns one of Gacy's paintings. Two businessmen eventually purchased many of John Wayne Gacy's prison paintings in the end and had them destroyed in a mass bonfire where people (including relatives of Gacy's victims) gathered and cheered.

RONNIE LEE GARDNER

CRIMES?

Ronnie Lee Gardner was born in Salt Lake City in 1961. Gardner, like many criminals and killers, had a dreadful childhood. He suffered abuse and neglect. Gardner was said to have got into drugs and alcohol by the time he was ten years-old. He was in and out of institutions as a teenager but eventually seemed to be getting on the right path when he attended industrial school and had some kids. Sadly though, the straight and narrow was a place that Ronnie Lee Gardner was never destined to reside. He landed in prison for robbery and proved to be an obstreperous inmate to say the least. In 1984 he faked illness and escaped from the University of Utah Hospital. One of the prison transportation officers was beaten so badly by Gardner in this escape that he needed extensive surgery on his face.

In October, 1984, Gardner robbed a bar in Salt Lake City. A bartender named Melvyn John Otterstrom was shot dead in the raid. Gardner was high on cocaine at the time. The robbery only netted a paltry amount of money. Ronnie Lee Gardner actually attended the funeral of Melvyn John Otterstrom by pretending to be a friend. In reality Gardner hadn't known Melvyn John Otterstrom from Adam - besides shooting him. It was a very weird and dark thing to do. Gardner was in police custody about three weeks after the murder. One of his accomplices (who was the getaway driver that night) is believed to have shopped Gardner to the authorities.

All hell broke loose during Gardner's trial because he was slipped a gun by an accomplice (it is believed the gun was hidden in a female washroom) and tried to escape. Gardner used people in the court as human shields. He was shot by one of the security guards but Gardner was still able to wound a bailiff and shoot attourney Michael Burdell in the eye. Burdell, who was a Vietnam veteran, died shortly afterwards after being taken to hospital.

Gardner actually managed to get outside but was then surrounded by cops so had to surrender. It later transpired that someone had also hidden a bag of men's clothing in the courthouse. Gardner clearly had accomplices and had been planning to escape. Darcy Perry McCoy and Carma Jolley Hainsworth were arrested for smuggling in the clothes but the identity of who supplied the gun was unknown.

Gardner pleaded guilty to the murder of Otterstrom. As you might imagine, security was very tight at this second attempt at a trial and the security guards watch Gardner like a hawk. Ronnie Lee Gardner had been diagnosed with a personality disorder and the jury was given the option of declaring this a case of manslaughter if they deemed that Gardner wasn't of sound mind. In the end they sentenced him to death.

Gardner was very young for someone on death row and also proved to be a pain in the neck for prison staff and officials. If there were any inmate protests or riots he was usually the ringleader. He once smashed in a glass barrier and had sex with a woman who had come to visit him. In 1994, Gardner violently stabbed another inmate with a knife he'd fashioned from some sunglasses. The victim received puncture wounds to the face and chest.

Under a quirk of the law in that state, Gardner was still able to choose his method of execution. He chose to be killed by firing squad - which was very rare and about to be phased out. After many appeals, Gardner was executed on June the 18th, 2010, by a firing squad at Utah State Prison in Draper.

Among the protestors outside were members of victim Michael Burdell's family. They said Michael was a pacifist who opposed the death penalty. Ronnie Lee Gardner offered no words before his execution and seemed calm. He was 49 years-old.

LAST MEAL?

For his last ever meal, Gardner asked for lobster tail and steak. He was yet another death row prisoner who loved steak. For his dessert Gardner went for a classic combination and had apple pie and vanilla ice cream. To wash down this meal he had some 7 Up. 7 Up is an American brand of lemon-lime-flavored non-caffeinated soft drink. 7 Up was invented in 1929. Gardner had one other (non food related) request for his last meal. He asked if he could watch the Lord of the Rings film trilogy while he ate. That must have been a seriously long meal because those movies go on forever!

ED GEIN

CRIMES?

Ed Gein was born in La Crosse County, Wisconsin, on August 27, 1906. It was Gein's proclivity for ghoulish grave robbing that made him infamous. Gein was especially close to his mother Augusta Wilhelmine - a bond that would leave him in a mentally fragile state when she died. The family lived on an isolated 155-acre farm in the town of Plainfield in Waushara County. Ed Gein, and his brother Henry only left the farm to go to school. Their mother was deeply religious and very strict. The two boys were not encouraged to make friends and had it drummed into them that the world was a wicked place they should avoid as much as possible (lest they be infected by its evil).

George Gein, the father, died in 1940. Ed and Henry had to do more on the farm after his death and Ed also picked up work as a sort of handyman around town. Ed Gein was considered to be rather odd by the locals but seemed essentially harmless. He was even used as a babysitter on occasion. Henry, in contrast to Ed, eventually started to find life on the farm dull

and constrictive. He had met a woman and planned on moving
out. Henry felt that Ed's relationship with their mother was
becoming unhealthy. In 1944 there was a mysterious tragedy
when Ed and Henry were burning vegetation on the farm and
Henry was later found dead. However, there were no burns on
his body. It was presumed to be heart failure or suffocation
from the fumes but - retrospectively - it seems very plausible
that Ed might have killed Henry.

Henry is said to have angered Ed by comments he made about
their mother - a fact which supplies the most likely motive.
Now it was just Ed Gein and his mother left on the farm. Gein
was devoted to his mother and waited on her hand and foot.
Her health began to collapse though and she endured a stroke.
Augusta Gein died in 1945 and Ed Gein was left alone on the
farm. He was absolutely devastated. Gein's already fragile
mental state rapidly deteriorated. He boarded up his mother's
rooms and the house began to grow increasingly dirty and
squalid. Gein found himself becoming fascinated with
gruesome pictures and Nazi imagery. He continued to work as
a handyman and even sold some land so money wasn't a huge
problem.

On the morning of November the 16th, 1957, Plainfield
hardware store owner Bernice Worden vanished. Her son,
Deputy Sheriff Frank Worden, entered her closed store and
found evidence of a robbery. The register was open and there
were signs of blood. Worden knew that one of the last
customers had been Ed Gein. He'd come in for some antifreeze
the night before and said he would return in the morning to
collect it. The police decided to visit the Gein farm and what
they found soon became one of the most macabre legends in
the history of crime.

Searching the property, they found Bernice Worden's
decapitated and mutilated body. The police also found human
skulls, bones, chairs made of human skin, female genitalia,
facemasks made from real faces, and all manner of gruesome
mementoes. Gein had been digging up bodies in the local

cemetery and mutilating them, using the skin to craft bizarre clothes, masks, and furniture. It was quite literally like something out of The Texas Chainsaw Massacre (which of course the Ed Gein story partly inspired).

Under questioning, Gein confessed to stealing nine bodies from the local graveyards. He had been trying to make a 'skin suit' to wear in a deranged bid to feel close to his late mother. Gein also told the police he had killed Mary Hogan, a woman who had been missing since 1954. The head of this woman was found on Gein's farm. The police who worked this case were deeply shocked and affected by the grisly discoveries. They would never forget the awful sights that greeted them on Gein's farm.

On November the 21st, 1957, Gein was arraigned on one count of first degree murder in Waushara County Court, where he pleaded not guilty by reason of insanity. Gein was diagnosed with schizophrenia and found mentally incompetent, thus unfit for trial. He was sent to the Central State Hospital for the Criminally Insane, a maximum-security facility in Waupun, Wisconsin, and later transferred to the Mendota State Hospital in Madison, Wisconsin. Gein's farm later burned down in what was believed to be an accident rather than deliberate. It was perhaps for the best. The prospect of the farm becoming some macabre 'sightseeing' tourist attraction was not something that the locals or the police relished. Gein died at the Mendota Mental Health Institute in 1984. He was 77. After he died, ghoulish memento collectors chipped away at his gravestone for keepsakes.

LAST MEAL?

The last thing Ed Gein ate before he was arrested by the police was porkchops, potatoes, macaroni, and pickles. This meal took place at the home of a neighbour. Ed didn't do much cooking at home because his farm had no electricity. This is why he liked to cadge homecooked meals off other people. When he was at home, Ed tended to eat oatmeal and stuff out of cans. He was a big fan of cookies too by all accounts - which probably isn't surprising because (graverobbing notwithstanding) he was a childlike sort of man in many ways. The last thing he ate before his death was some chicken noodle soup at the Mendota Mental Health Institute. Despite his notorious and grisly reputation, Ed Gein's dietary habits were relatively normal - all things considering.

HARVEY GLATMAN

CRIMES?

Harvey Glatman was born in New York in 1927. Glatman was a killer active in the 1950s. He is believed to have killed four women and is known as The Glamour Girl Slayer or The Lonely-Hearts Killer. Glatman would pretend to be a photographer to lure victims. He would then rape and murder them. When he was caught, the police found a toolbox that Glatman used to store disturbing photographs of his bound victims. As a child, Glatman was said to find it sexually exciting to try and suffocate himself. He said he was always obsessed by bondage and ropes. When he was in high school he once tied up one of his classmates and molested her.

Glatman was a thief as a young adult but continued to commit sex crimes and wound up in prison for some short spells. In 1957 he moved to Los Angeles and became a TV repair man. Glatman's dark desires though had not gone away. He was a rather small and goofy looking young man who was always frustrated by his lack of success with women. Glatman decided that he would pose as a photographer who did glamour shots (for things like lurid paperback covers) and this would be his passport to meet beautiful women. However, he didn't simply want to photograph the women. He wanted to rape and kill them too.

His first victim was 19-year-old model Judy Ann Dull. Dull thought she was being paid $50 to pose for the cover of a pulp novel. It is speculated that because Glatman was a very small man (who looked much younger than his actual age) his victims never detected any threat from him until it was too late. Glatman took Dull to his apartment where he raped her at gunpoint. He then drove her out to the desert and strangled her to death. At the apartment, Glatman also took photographs of Dull with her hands, feet, and mouth bound by rope. This would be a consistent theme in his murders.

His next victim was Shirley Ann Bridgeford. Bridgeford was a young woman that Glatman had made contact with through a lonely hearts ad. They arranged to meet to go to a dance but instead Glatman repeated what he had done with his first victim. He raped Shirley Ann Bridgeford at gunpoint and took photographs of her tied up. He then took her out to the desert and killed her.

Glatman's third victim was Ruth Mercado. This time he was back to his photographer deception. Ruth was booked for a photo session by Glatman. She actually cancelled the session because she didn't feel very well that day but Glatman, now knowing where she lived, broke into her house and raped her. He then, as was his usual custom, took her out to the desert.

"She was one I really liked," said Glatman. "So I told her we were going out to a deserted spot where we wouldn't be bothered while I took more pictures. We drove out to the Escondido district and spent most of the day out on the desert. I took a lot more pictures and tried and tried to figure out how to keep from killing her. But I couldn't come up with any answer."

Glatman's killing spree was ended by 28-year-old model Lorraine Vigil. Vigil got in a car with Glatman to head for an arranged photoshoot but she became suspicious when she noticed that he seemed to be going in the wrong direction. When she challenged him he tried to pull out a gun and the pair began grappling. Glatman was forced to pull over and the commotion was thankfully enough to attract the attention of the public and (eventually) the police. A patrol officer soon arrived on the scene and arrested Glatman.

Glatman made no attempt to deny his guilt and confessed to the murders. The police were directed to the box where he kept the photographs of his bound victims. In addition to his three murders, Glatman is a suspect in the murder of 'Boulder Jane Doe,' a victim whose body was discovered by hikers near Boulder, Colorado in 1954. Glatman pled guilty at his trial and seemed to desire the death penalty. He got his wish. Glatman was given the death sentence and killed in the gas chamber of San Quentin State Prison in 1959.

LAST MEAL?

The thought of being killed made no difference to the appetite of Glatman. He actually had two hearty meals before his final curtain call.

The night before his execution, Glatman was afforded a special meal of shrimp cocktail, rare T-bone steak, and French fries. Prawn cocktail, also known as shrimp cocktail, is a seafood dish consisting of shelled, cooked prawns in a Marie Rose sauce or cocktail sauce, served in a glass. Prawn cocktail has probably gone out of fashion a bit these days but it was a trendy sort of starter in its day.

Glatman had a banana split for dessert and washed his meal down with soda. The next morning, the day of the execution, Glatman then had a cooked breakfast of eggs, bacon, toast, and orange juice.

If nothing else, Harvey Glatman certainly didn't go to the gas chamber on an empty stomach.

GESCHE GOTTFRIED

CRIMES?

Gesche Gottfried was born born Gesche Margarethe Timm in Germany in 1831. She was known as The Angel of Bremen and poisoned fifteen people to death. It made no difference to Gottfried who the person was. She happily poisoned friends and relatives. Gesche Gottfried grew up in a large and poor family and always felt rather unloved. It is speculated that she later developed Munchausen syndrome by proxy (MSP). In medical terms, this is defined as a disorder in which the caretaker of a person either makes up fake symptoms or causes real symptoms to make it appear as though the person is injured or ill. The term by proxy means through a substitute.

Though MSP is primarily a mental illness, it is also considered a form of abuse. Many people with MSP exaggerate or lie about a person's symptoms to get attention. They may also create symptoms by poisoning food, withholding food, or causing an infection. Some people may even have a person undergo painful or risky tests and procedures to try to gain sympathy from their family members or community.

Gesche Gottfried poisoned to death, amongst others, two husbands, her mother and father, two daughters and a son, her brother, a fiancé, and numerous friends. She enjoyed the sympathy that people gave her as a result of these deaths. They obviously had no idea that Gottfried was killing these people so showered her with sympathy and support each time she 'suffered' the loss of a presumed loved one. She would mix rat poison in animal fat and then slip this into the food of her victims. She often killed people slowly by giving them small amounts of poison at a time. Once the victim started to become ill, Gottfriend would of course volunteer to care for them.

Part of the motivation for these murders was obviously money as Gesche collected a number of inheritances as a result of so many relatives dying. She was creative with her methods and once poisoned someone through a dish of shellfish. Her exploits came to an end when one would be victim noticed some white power on food that Gesche had given him. He consulted a local doctor about this and the substance was identified as arsenic. Gesche was arrested in 1828. She was 43 years-old at the time. Gesche Gottfried was sentenced to death by decapitation and beheaded on April the 21st 1831. This was the last public execution ever carried out in the city of Bremen.

LAST MEAL?

There was evidently no last meal custom in Bremen for Gesche Gottfried to enjoy. She was though offered some red wine just before she died. Gottfried took a few calming sips of this wine and then readied herself to face execution.

THOMAS J. GRASSO

CRIMES?

Thomas J. Grasso was born in 1962. Grasso was a thief and killer - and a ruthless and heartless one too. Grasso tended to choose elderly and vulnerable people as victims. In 1990, Grasso strangled 87 year-old Hilda Johnson to death in her Tulsa home on Christmas Eve. He used Johnson's Christmas lights to strangle her. Grasso found only ten dollars in the house so he took the television set - which he sold for $125. Slim pickings for a brutal murder. So much for Christmas spirit! Grasso had not an ounce of humanity.

Less than a year later, Grasso murdered 81 year-old Leslie Holtz in New York. Grasso stole Holtz's social security cheque after the murder. His targeting of frail and elderly victims was thoroughly despicable. Grasso was an evil coward. The most senseless thing about these awful murders is that he wasn't even getting away with much money anyway. it's not as if these elderly victims were rich.

Thankfully, Grasso was pretty easy to catch in the end. Within two weeks of his last murder he was a person of interest to the police and he confessed very quickly to the previous murder too once they spoke to him and subjected him to questioning. Grasso was extradited to Oklahoma and sentenced to death. There was a bit of a bunfight between jurisdictions for custody of Grasso and his fate become bound up in politics.

Certain politicians (especially those facing an imminent election) love having someone to execute because it makes them look tough on crime (American politicians tend to greatly fear being seen as soft on crime because they think it will lose them votes). Grasso was eventually was killed by lethal injection in 1995. As far as death row goes, the time between his arrest and execution was fairly short compared to other cases. Five years on death row is surprisingly modest in terms of duration.

LAST MEAL?

For his last meal, Grasso requested steamed mussels and steamed clams. He was YET another killer with a fondness for seafood. He also requested barbecue spare ribs and a double cheeseburger from Burger King. Burger King describe this as two signature flame-grilled beef patties topped with melted American cheese, crinkle cut pickles, yellow mustard, and ketchup on a toasted sesame seed bun.

Grasso wasn't finished yet though. He also had pumpkin pie (maybe Glatman loved Halloween?) with strawberries and cream and two strawberry milkshakes. Grasso was clearly a big fan of strawberries. Grasso also requested a can of Spaghetti-Os. Spaghetti-Os is an American brand of canned ring-shaped pasta pieces in tomato sauce. It is what you might describe as a quick and convenient sort of comfort food (sort of like baked beans in Britain). However, the prison authorities failed to supply a can of Spaghetti-Os and gave him some spaghetti instead. Maybe something was lost in translation.

Grasso was rather annoyed by this mix-up. As he headed towards his imminent date with a lethal injection his last ever words on planet Earth were - "I did not get my Spaghetti-Os, I got spaghetti! I want the press to know this!" Still fuming at being denied a can of Spaghetti-Os, Thomas J. Grasso was finally executed.

FRITZ HAARMANN

CRIMES?

Fritz Haarmann was born in Hanover, Germany in 1879. In true crime circles he is known as The Vampire of Hanover. Haarmann was an unhappy child (what else is new when it comes to serial killers?) and seemed to have a lifelong bitterness at his father. He suffered seizures when he was a boy and it is speculated that these might have left some lasting damage that impaired his mental health. He went to a military academy (in those days Germany was a very militaristic nation) but was kicked out because they didn't think he was healthy enough to make a good student or potential soldier.

After this, Haarmann got married (although he was secretly gay) and picked up some work at a shipping docks. Money was still tight though and he became a petty thief - which earned him a short spell in prison. It was after his release from prison that Haarmann seemed to completely snap and become a deranged serial killer. His victims were the usual serial killer targets. Prostitutes, runaways, homeless people. All of his victims were boys or men. Haarmann would lure the victims back to his home with promises of food and drink. When they

were vulnerable he would bite them in the throat in savage
fashion. He referred to this as a 'love bite'. If this 'love bite'
hadn't killed them then Haarmann would finish them off by
strangulation.

Haarmann would keep any possessions his victims had and
sell them on the black market. This wasn't the only thing he
sold on the black market. He also sold meat. Could this meat
have been the human flesh of his victims? That doesn't seem
unlikely at all. Fritz Haarmann was no rocket scientist when it
came to brains though. He wasn't exactly the most adept serial
killer when it came to covering the tracks of his grisly deeds.
Haarmann had been dumping his victims in the Leine River (a
river in Thuringia and Lower Saxony). Some of the bodies
washed ashore - which led the police to investigate the river
thoroughly.

They dragged the river and found hundreds of human bones.
From what they found the police estimated that there were
over twenty victims at least in this river. Haarmann, because
of his criminal history, ended up on a list of suspects and was
placed under secret observation by the police. They saw him
trying to pick up boys at the train station and decided to
search his home. Haarmann's home was full of blood stains
and he was swiftly arrested. The trial of Fritz Haarmann took
place in 1924. It didn't last very long. He was found guilty of
24 murders and sentenced to death by beheading.

LAST MEAL?

There was evidently no food on offer for Fritz Haarmann but
he still had a couple of requests though. Fritz Haarmann
simply asked for a cup of coffee and a Cuban cigar. Cuban
cigars are famed around the world for their quality. Fritz
Haarmann's requests were granted and he enjoyed one last
cigar before the final curtain finally fell on this strange and
wicked life.

ANNA MARIE HAHN

CRIMES?

Anna Marie Hahn was born Anna Marie Filse in Bavaria, Germany, in 1906. When she was still a teenager, Hahn had a child and claimed the father was a respected doctor. However, this respected doctor did not exist. It was something Hahn had made up to mitigate the stigma of being a single mother. Hahn's pregnancy with no marriage or husband was something of a scandal in the family and she was sent away to the United States in 1929. Anna Marie Hahn's family was fairly rich and conservative so you could say that they rather sent her into exile. She had become the black sheep of the clan.

Anna Marie ended up in Cincinnati, Ohio where she married a fellow German immigrant named Philip Hahn. They started a family together. Anna Marie is said to have briefly run a bakery but clearly didn't enjoy this much and it didn't last very long. Accounts of her life often say she had a number of gambling debts. One thing was certain in the end. Anna Marie Hahn liked money and would do literally anything to get her hands on it.

Alarm bells regarding the activities of Anna Marie first began to ring when she seemed unusually insistent that her husband should take out life insurance - despite the fact that he was quite young. Sure enough, her husband soon fell ill and was carted off to hospital (where he managed to survive) by relatives. With her marriage in tatters, Anna Marie took up a position caring for elderly men in Cincinnati's German community. You can probably guess what happened next. That's right. The elderly patients she was caring for soon began to suddenly and mysteriously die.

Anna Marie would borrow money from her patients before they died. One patient even left her a house in his will. She would earn their trust (and in some cases it seems even they love) before she poisoned them. The last victim was George Obendoerfer in 1937. Anna Marie plundered his bank account after she'd killed him. The police got suspicious of Anna Marie because of the bank transfer she had arranged so soon after the death of Obendoerfer. His body was found to contain poison - as were the bodies of her previous two patients after exhumations.

It transpired that Hahn was creative in her methods and used different poisons (including arsenic and croton oil) on different victims. A search of her home found a large stash of poison (in addition to belongings she had stolen from her victims) and she was taken into custody. After a four week trial, Anna Marie was sentenced to death. This came as a big shock to her. Anna Marie Hahn had been so confident of a not guilty verdict that she had her bags packed so that she was ready to go home. At the trial Anna Marie Hahn was cogent and well dressed and insisted she was innocent. The evidence though said otherwise.

As her execution loomed, Anna Marie became confessional and composed a written statement. 'God above will tell me what made me do these terrible things,' she wrote. 'I couldn't have been in my right mind when I did them. I loved all people so much. Now I am so close to death. Death is all around me. I have been here (on death row) for what seems another lifetime already. Several other people in this place have been called out. I hope that God will take care of my son, for I would not want anything to happen to my boy. I feel that God has shown me my wrongs in life and my only regret is that I have not the power to undo the trouble and heartache that I have caused.'

Anna Marie Hahn was executed by electrocution at the Ohio Penitentiary on December the 7th, 1938. Her son Oskar was given a new identity and served in the United States Navy during World War 2.

LAST MEAL?

We don't know what Anna Marie Hahn had for her last meal or if she even had a last meal but we do know that just before her execution she invited some journalists into the prison for an interview and some cake and punch. Presumably then the cake WAS her last meal? Hmmn. I don't know about you but I think I'd be somewhat reluctant to tuck into a cake that had been supplied by Anna Marie Hahn! I wouldn't imagine too many of those reporters willingly sampled either the cake or the punch.

JOHN HAIGH

CRIMES?

John George Haigh was born in Lincolnshire in 1909. Haigh was a British serial killer known as The Acid Bath Murderer. He killed at least six people but (as ever with serial killers) the real body count might be higher. Haigh was basically a thief and conman who became inspired by the tale of Georges-Alexandre Sarret, a French killer who used sulphuric acid to dispose of victims. Haigh simply deduced that if he killed the people he had robbed and conned and dissolved their bodies in acid then no one would ever be able to finger him for any crimes.

To test his dark theory, Haigh murdered a man and seized the man's bank savings and pension. He even sold the victim's house. The victim was William McSwan - a former employer of Haigh. Haigh was jealous of McSwan's luxury lifestyle and this was the motivation for the murder. He murdered McSwan by clubbing him over the head and dissolved the body in a vat of acid. When the parents of William McSwan became suspicious of their son's disappearance and asked Haigh about his whereabouts he killed them too in similar fashion.

Haigh was said to have run up large gambling debts around this time and, needing more money to fund his lifestyle, he decided to kill again. His targets this time were Dr Archibald Henderson and his wife Rose. Haigh stole a revolver from Henderson and used it to shoot both of them dead. Haigh then dissolved them in acid and sold all of their possessions. He did though keep their dog and car for himself.

There were six verified victims of Haigh in all but he is believed to have killed as many as nine people. He would move around a lot and often stay in hotels. When money became tight again he would simply look for some new wealthy victims to kill so that he could ransack their property and bank accounts. Haigh was very crafty and would often forge legal documents from his victims handing over their houses and finances to him.

John George Haigh was undone because of his past convictions for theft and fraud. When the police decided to investigate him in relation to some recent crimes they found that Haigh now lived in rooms with no drain access. Haigh had dissolved his latest victim in acid but then covered it in rubble (rather than dispose of it down the drain). The rubble was rather suspicious and the police investigated and thus revealed the dark secret of John Haigh.

The police proved there was human fat and remains in the rubble and - as a consequence - Haigh was sentenced to death and hung in 1949. The police actually found part of a foot in the rubble. Before he was hung, Haigh confessed to a number of murders which could never be verified because there was (obviously, given his strategy of dissolving victims in acid) no actual evidence or remains. His other victims are alleged to include two women.

LAST MEAL?

The death penalty in Britain was abolished many decades ago but when it was still part of the criminal system the 'death row last meal' custom we are familiar with from the United States was not really a tradition in British prisons. It was apparently quite common though for the condemned prisoner to be offered a nip of alcohol before their execution. This is the opposite to the American death row custom - where you are permitted to order a special meal but you are NOT allowed to have any alcohol. Haigh, urbane to the end, asked for a large brandy before his execution. After this last drink he was ready to face the final curtain. John Haigh's gloves and apron (which he used to protect himself from burns from the acid bath) were later displayed at New Scotland Yard's infamous Black Museum.

Garlic Bread

ROBERT ALTON HARRIS

CRIMES?

Robert Alton Harris was born in North Carolina in 1953. Harris was a bad egg from the get go and in and out of prison as a young man. You didn't need to be Nostradamus to predict that he was going to do something really awful in the end. His main sideline was car theft but he also had a rap for manslaughter. The manslaughter charge came when Harris beat a man to death. He alleged that he had done this to protect the man's wife. The court established though that this wasn't the case and Harris had beaten the man to death for no particular reason. Robert Alton Harris was simply a sadistic bully and habitual criminal.

In 1979, the 25 year-old Harris and his brother decided (as you do) to rob a bank in San Diego. They stole a car to use for this bank raid. Two sixteen year-old boys were in the car at the time. Robert Alton Harris heartlessly shot both of the boys dead and then proceeded with his bank raid as planned. The two boys, John Mayeski and Michael Baker, were celebrating one of them getting their driving licence and were about to go fishing for the day.

Robert Alton Harris took the boys to a quiet spot and shot them multiple times. He then went back to the car and finished the cheeseburgers the murdered boys had been eating. Words cannot describe how evil and emotionless Robert Alton Harris was. Harris then stole $2,000 from the bank but was arrested only an hour after the raid. One of the police officers who arrested him was the father of one of the boys Harris had just murdered. The officer didn't know this at the time though - which is probably just as well. Who knows how he might have reacted had he known?

On March the 6th, 1979, Robert Harris was convicted in the San Diego County Superior Court of two counts of murder in the first degree with special circumstances as well as two counts of kidnapping, and was sentenced to death. His brother was convicted of kidnapping and got six years. The defence team of Harris argued that he was born premature with a brain impairment and this should be taken into account. This was basically their main tactic in trying to avoid the death sentence.

A surprisingly high number of killers received head injuries from an accident in their childhood or youth. There is a theory that this impairs the part of the brain responsible for ruminating on the consequences of one's actions. Richard Ramirez suffered two head injuries as a child. It is believed they left him with seizures. Nannie Doss (aka The Giggling Granny) suffered a head injury as a child when she was involved in an accident where an iron bar flew off a train and struck her. Doss tried to use this head injury as a defence for her murders. Fred West, who was one of the worst serial killers in British history, suffered two head injuries as a teenager when he was involved in a motorcycle crash and then later fell from a fire escape.

There are a large number of other examples of killers suffering a blow to the head at a young age. Now, this obviously does not explain all the killers who didn't suffer head injuries but it certainly might have been a factor in those who DID. The legal team of Robert Alton Harris were ultimately unsuccessful though in avoiding the death penalty. After the usual battery of endless appeals and legal delays, Robert Alton Harris was executed on April the 21st, 1992, in the gas chamber at San Quentin State Prison.

LAST MEAL?

Harris went for a conventional junk food blowout when it came to his last meal. There was nothing fancy or obtuse about his request at all. He requested a 21-piece bucket of Kentucky Fried Chicken to begin with. There are well over 3000 calories in a giant bucket of KFC but it seems highly unlikely that Harris managed to eat it all. He hardly needed to watch his waistline anymore though did he?

Robert Alton Harris then requested two large Domino's pizzas but then changed his mind regarding the pizza and asked for Tombstone Pizza instead. Tombstone is a brand of frozen pizza. It is available with a variety of toppings and is generally considered to be a good product. Harris washed his meal down

with Pepsi and simply asked for some jelly beans when it came
to afters. Jelly beans are small bean-shaped sugar candies with
soft candy shells and thick gel interiors. After all that KFC and
pizza it is probably not a surprise that Harris didn't have much
room left for a pudding. He also requested a packet of Camel
cigarettes. The prison waived the usual rules and let him have
some cigarettes.

ADOLF HITLER

CRIMES?

A man who needs no introduction, it is hard to know where to
begin with Hitler's crimes. Adolf Hitler was the dictator of
Nazi Germany during the war and the man responsible for the
conflict. He is remembered as one of the most evil men in
history and was responsible for the deaths of millions. Hitler
was Austrian but became a staunch German patriot. He served
in World War I as a runner between trenches and also
experienced life as an impoverished and failed artist. Hitler
was left with a deep and enduring bitterness when Germany
lost the First World War and - a bigot and racist - he also
harboured a hatred of Jewish people (who he scapegoated for
Germany's problems).

After the war Hitler led the National Socialist German
Workers Party and after years of struggle helped by the
troubles of post-war Germany (which felt humiliated by the
terms of her defeat in the war and had suffered from poverty
and hyper-inflation) he became Chancellor in 1933. Despite
vague early mumblings about working with other parties the
Nazis soon exerted an iron grip on the country and Hitler
began to plot expansionist policies based on his belief that
Germany needed to right what he saw as the wrongs of the
Versailles Treaty and secure "living space" for its people. What
Hitler wanted was a German administered Europe that

essentially existed as a Nazi Empire based on his racist ideology.

Hitler's racial persecution saw an estimated 11 million people taken to concentration camps and murdered. In addition to the murder of Jews, Nazi Germany killed Slavs, Gypsies, gay people, and the disabled and mentally ill. Hitler placed the processing of these orders in the hands of powerful Nazis like Himmler and Heydrich. Despite peddling fanatical nonsense about the 'master race', the leading Nazis were a bizarre and sickly bunch. Hitler was beset with medical ailments, Goebbels was short with a club foot, and Himmler was a disconcertingly odd looking man with bad eyesight.

After the early successes of the military campaign, Hitler's confidence turned out to be completely misplaced and, after the debacle at Stalingrad, Nazi Germany found itself fighting a costly war of attrition that it did not have the manpower or industrial resources to win. Near the end of the war, Hitler and his closest circle retreated to his claustrophobic, damp, but heavily fortified bunker in Berlin. The endless massed tanks and soldiers of the Red Army were within sight of Berlin with only some hopelessly outgunned and outnumbered German forces, including Hitler Youth, between them and the bunker.

Hitler's bunker shook and rattled with dust as the shells and air raids continued from both the Allies and the Red Army. The war is lost but, trapped in this surreal atmosphere, Hitler fluctuated between rage and optimism. He gave operational orders to German Armies that actually ceased to exist weeks ago but still appear on his battle maps. Hitler was planning the defence of Berlin with phantom divisions. The last footage taken of Hitler was him meeting some Hitler Youth boys outside his bunker. Hitler looks like a broken man. He is stooped and aged and he can't stop one of his hands from shaking. Many believe Hitler had Parkinsons.

Hitler's quack personal physician Theodor Morell played a big part in the rapid deterioration of Hitler's health. Morell injected Hitler with prescriptions that included arsenic, strychnine, and various unknown drugs. Hitler's health wasn't helped much either by the fact that he lived in a bunker and rarely got any sleep. Hitler committed suicide on the 30th of April 1945 after marrying Eva Braun (who then killed herself with a cyanide capsule). Hitler shot himself with a Walther PPK - the gun later used by James Bond. His body was the taken out into the bunker garden and burned - as per his instructions.

LAST MEAL?

Hitler was famously a vegetarian - though some historians have disputed this. One of his cooks is alleged to have given him meat based gravy. Hitler's favourite food was said to be mashed potato with fried eggs. He ate a lot of rice and pasta and he always enjoyed a simple salad of lettuce with lemon juice. Hitler apparently loved mushrooms too. At his military compounds there was always a greenhouse and garden so that fresh vegetables were available to him. Hitler had his own personal baker too so that fresh bread was always on the menu.

Hitler was thought to have adopted his almost teetotal, vegetarian, non-smoking lifestyle in the 1920's when the Nazi party was becoming more popular. This was because of health reasons as Hitler had digestive problems and would sweat if he ate meat or drank too much. Hitler was committed to his cause and saw a healthier diet as helping him have more energy for his political work.

A German soldier who was present at one of Hitler's meals later wrote that the dictator had terrible table manners. The soldier said that Hitler ate rapidly and kept picking his nose. Hitler had a team of young women who had to test his food to make sure it hadn't been poisoned. If the women ate the food and showed no ill effects for an hour the food was deemed safe and served to Hitler. Hitler wasn't much of a breakfast person by all accounts. He would get up very late and usually just have bread and marmalade.

Hitler had a sweet tooth and ate a lot of chocolate and cakes. It probably explains why he had trouble with his teeth. Hitler had such a sweet tooth that he would put sugar in a glass of wine. The teahouse on the Mooslahnerkopf hill was often frequented by Adolf Hitler when he was at his Berghof at Obersalzberg. Hitler's secretary said that he would always order apple pie and that he preferred cocoa to tea or coffee. Another staple on the Hitler menu was soup. He loved soup. Constanze Manziarly, who was Hitler's last cook, said the final meal he ate in the bunker before he shot himself was some pasta in a light tomato sauce. Hitler's cook was preparing creamed potatoes and eggs for him when she was informed that he was dead.

There is a surprisingly enduring conspiracy theory that Hitler didn't kill himself but instead faked his own death. The theory that Hitler was smuggled out of Berlin to South America on a U-boat and spent the last years of his life living in Argentina has spawned a number of books and TV shows. The Allied authorities kept an open mind on this theory themselves for a time when the war had ended. However, the evidence for this theory is scant to say the least. The theory states that Hitler was smuggled to the Spanish coast and taken to Argentina on a U-boat. From all that we know about Hitler, he didn't exactly seem like the sort of person who would shave his hair off and go and live in the jungle as a fugitive!

H.H. HOLMES

CRIMES?

H. H. Holmes (born as Herman Webster Mudgett but better known as Henry Howard Holmes) was born in Gilmanton, New Hampshire in 1861. H.H. Holmes is often dubbed

America's first serial killer. In the 1890s, he constructed a 'murder castle' above his drug store. This was a windowless room where he could torture and murder. The childhood of Holmes is somewhat vague in that there are conflicting reports of how bad it was or indeed wasn't. There seems to be no clear consensus.

Holmes attended various colleges as a teenager and got booted out of one of these schools for theft. In 1882 he entered University of Michigan's Department of Medicine and Surgery and managed to graduate in the end. Holmes later confessed to the murder of a medical school colleague as part of an insurance scam. By this time he had married and become a father - although he was said to treat his wife badly (he apparently even got married to another woman without bothering to get divorced) and they soon became estranged.

Holmes moved to New York and there was a curious incident where he was seen with a little boy who then seemed to vanish. Holmes appeared to flee from the area before this matter could be investigated. Holmes drifted around at this point and took a number of jobs. He was a compulsive fraudster and was also involved in the suspicious death of a boy at a drugstore. It was around this time that he changed his name to Henry Howard Holmes in an attempt to evade past deeds. In 1886 he arrived in Chicago and got a job in a drugstore - which he eventually purchased. He then bought a property across the road which he planned to turn into a drugstore and apartment building. There were even plans for it to serve as a hotel.

The building was full of mazes and secret rooms and various 'chutes' and contraptions to dispose of bodies. Many women were seen going into the building but few came out again. Holmes tended to murder for financial gain and took out insurance on a number of victims. Holmes had an accomplice named Benjamin Piteze in his frauds and deadly deeds. The capture of H.H Holmes was rather knotty and slow. He was wanted for arson and so fled with the intention of creating another 'Murder Castle' elsewhere. He was eventually arrested in Boston in connection with a horse swindle.

When the police investigated his Murder Castle they found a large number of bodies but decomposition made it difficult to say how many victims there were. Holmes confessed to over thirty murders but true figure is almost certainly considerably higher than that. He was an absolutely ruthless man who was perfectly willing to kill women, children, business associates, and generally anyone. On May 7, 1896, Holmes was hanged at Moyamensing Prison. There is a theory that H.H. Holmes could have been Jack the Ripper but the evidence is vague at best. The vast geographical distance between the two sets of murders alone makes it highly unlikely.

LAST MEAL?

There was a very plain last meal for the dreaded H. H. Holmes before his date with the gallows. He had boiled eggs, plain toast and a cup of coffee. This sounds a lot like a standard prison breakfast so it seems unlikely that Holmes was afforded any whimsical last request when it came to grub. You can't imagine that an educated wealth obsessed man like Holmes would have willingly chosen boiled eggs and toast as his last meal on planet Earth! One suspects he would have gone something a bit more fancy and sophisticated if given a choice.

SADDAM HUSSEIN

CRIMES?

Saddam Hussein, with his trademark mustache, served as the fifth president of Iraq from 1979 until 2003. He was one of the famous dictators in the world. Hussein invaded neighbours, started wars, had political opponents killed, and used chemical weapons on his own citizens. Suffice to say, he wasn't a terribly nice chap.

After the 2003 invasion of Iraq by the West (basically the United States, Britain and Australia - the rest of the world decided to keep their nose out of this controversial invasion), Saddam's regime was overthrown and he went into hiding. He was eventually found living in an underground hole on a farm. On the 5th of November 2006, Saddam was convicted by an Iraqi court of crimes against humanity and sentenced to death by hanging. He was executed on the 30th of December 2006. It was not a very dignified end. As he was hung, onlookers shouted abuse and filmed the execution on their telephones.

LAST MEAL?

There are conflicting accounts of what this famous despot had as his last meal. It is generally written that he had chicken and rice and a glass of water sweetened with honey. This was said to be Saddam's favourite grub. The Daily Mirror newspaper reported though that Saddam ate nothing but burgers and fries in the last days before his demise. This claim is probably taken with a pinch of salt.

Not that Saddam didn't have a penchant for Western food though. He was famously a big fan of the Quality Street chocolate selection confectionery brand. Quality Street has long been a Christmas staple in Britain. The dictator also had a stash of Mars Bars in his underground hole when he was found.

Saddam's favourite other foods were olives, shrimps, and lobster. He was said to be very partial to a glass of camel's milk - especially at breakfast. Meal times for a dictator are no (ahem) picnic though. Saddam was paranoid about enemies and had to have a number of food tasters sample his grub before he'd eat anything. His food had to be checked for radiation and poison. It is said that Saddam was quite fond of cooking for himself. That was very sensible because that way he could at least be sure that the food was safe.

BOBBY JOE LONG

CRIMES?

Bobby Joe Long was born in 1953 in Kenova, West Virginia. As a child he had some of the classic early tropes we see in many serial killers. He suffered a head injury and had a very dysfunctional relationship with his mother. Long also had Klinefelter syndrome - a condition which results in excessive estrogen production and gives males female characteristics. Long developed large breasts as a youngster and had to have surgery. As you might imagine, this condition made him something of a figure of ridicule amongst cruel boys at school.

Long got married in 1974 and had some children but the marriage didn't last long. As a young man he ticked that other familiar serial killer trope in that he was a compulsive rapist. Long was said to put classified ads in magazines and then rape and rob the women who answered the ads and met up with him. He worked as an X-ray technologist during the day but his secret life was dark indeed and something that he couldn't seem to control. His murder spree took place in the Tampa area.

Most of his victims were prostitutes or strippers he met in a bar. Once he got them home he would tie them up and rape them. His methods of murder were strangulation and slashing with a knife. Like many serial killers, he would leave his victims in explicit poses. A number of serial killers leave the bodies of victims in shocking or strange poses for the police or public to find. This would appear to be a case of the killer enjoying the dominance and control they have exerted over a victim. Serial killers seem to enjoy the thought of leaving a 'shocking' crime scene for the relatives and authorities to discover.

Long would usually dump the victims in somewhat out of the

way places like orange groves. Long stole the jewellery of his victims and sold it in Tampa pawn shops. The motivation for these murders was sexual but the secondary financial perks of murder were clearly not wasted on Long. Thankfully, Long didn't take too long to capture. He was not the most careful killer and left a raft of forensic evidence in his wake.

After some initial stonewalling in custody, Long confessed to eight murders. He was eventually convicted of more than that. Long was given the death penalty in 1985 before the usual series of appeals began. However, he was eventually executed in the end in 2019 by lethal injection. He was 65 years-old at the time of his death.

LAST MEAL?

Bobby Joe Long was evidently not much of a gourmet. He simply asked for some roast beef and bacon when it came to his last meal. That wasn't too much of a stretch for the prison kitchen you'd imagine. Long also requested some French fries. This meal was clearly more than enough for him because he didn't bother with dessert. He washed this all down with some soda. Long ate this final meal at 9-30 in the morning before he shuffled off this mortal coil by way of lethal injection. He had spent 34 years on death row. Long was the first death warrant signed by Gov. Ron DeSantis.

PETER KURTEN

CRIMES?

Peter Kürten was born in Cologne, Germany, in 1883. He is known as The Vampire of Dusseldorf. Kürten had a dreadful childhood thanks to a brutal alcoholic father and the grim poverty in which the family lived. The 1988 publication Sexual Homicide, Patterns and Motives said that 70% of families who raised a serial killer have had a history of alcohol abuse. It seems to a recurring pattern too that many serial killers were beaten and verbally abused by strict fathers.

Kürten suffered sexual abuse and is also said to have developed a liking for bestiality in his younger years. Kürten claimed that when he was nine he drowned two children by holding their heads underwater. He was constantly in and out of prison but committed awful crimes whenever he was released. He sexually abused and killed children (though was clearly never pegged for these crimes at the time). Kürten served in World War I but apparently deserted and fled. His main killing spree began in 1929. He targeted people regardless of age and would often frenziedly stab them dozens of times with scissors. He would sexually abuse dead bodies and found this very exciting.

Kürten loved the thought that his murders were attracting attention. He found it a great thrill to think that he was shocking and disgusting people. He even tried to nail one victim to a tree for the police to find but couldn't lift her because she was too heavy. In addition to stabbings, he often attacked victims with a hammer. Kürten was one of those vain serial killers who liked to toy with the police by sending them cryptic letters. We don't know exactly how many people he killed but he is believed to have attempted to murder over thirty people.

Kürten was captured because he'd let too many people escape - most saliently Maria Budlick, a woman he had raped. She survived this ordeal and went to the police. Kürten then did something rather clever. He confessed to his wife (believe it or he was actually married) and arranged it so that she would turn him in and claim the reward for his capture! It was Kürten's way of making sure his wife would be financially secure after his arrest.

Kürten did a series of lengthy interviews where he confessed his crimes to a famous psychologist named Professor Karl

Berg. This confession was later published as a book called The Sadist. Peter Kürten's trial began in 1931. Those in court were rather surprised to see this infamous monster in the flesh. He looked more like a mild mannered clerk than a serial killer. Peter Kürten was found guilty of murder and attempted murder and executed by guillotine on 2 July 1931.

LAST MEAL?

For his last meal before execution, Peter Kürten asked for a Wiener schnitzel. A Wiener Schnitzel is a cutlet of veal pounded thin by a meat tenderiser, then dipped in flour, egg and breadcrumbs, and fried until golden. Wiener schnitzel is considered to be one of the national dishes of Austria.

As a side dish, Kürten had some fried potatoes. To wash down this last meal, Kürten requested a bottle of white wine. Kürten was said to be quite chatty and unperturbed as he went to the guillotine. He genuinely loved the sound of his own voice and rarely shut up - even in these dire circumstances.

Believe it or not, Peter Kürten's head was once displayed at Ripley's Believe It or Not in Wisconsin Dells. The blurb went like this -

'Beheaded murderer Peter Kurten had his head bisected and mummified in attempt by scientists to understand the workings of his mind. Tried for 68 ghoulish crimes, including 9 murders, Peter Kurten was sentenced to be beheaded in Germany in 1931.

 So demented was Kurten's behavior, criminologists believed his brain had to be physically different from the norm in order for him to have concocted his grisly crimes. Therefore, his head was bisected to study his brain and the skull's internal cavities.'

WILLIAM LITTLE

CRIMES?

William Little was born in 1960. In 1983, Little murdered 23 year-old Marilyn Peters at her rural Texas home. Little worked as a roofer and was unusual when it came to killers in that he'd had no previous prison convictions (though this might be explained by the fact that he was still very young). Peters was raped and then stabbed around twenty times with a knife. Once she was dead, Little then had sex with the corpse. It was a ghastly and horrendous murder. Necrophilia is a common postmortem activity for sexual killers because it doesn't give the victim the opportunity reject the offender.

'Necrophilia,' wrote sciencedirect.com, 'is a term derived from the Greek words philios (attraction to/love) and nekros (dead body) and involves the sexual attraction to a dead body. Surprisingly, necrophilia dates back hundreds of years and has been documented in Greek mythology, ancient cultures, the Greco-Roman period, the middle ages, and in the modern era. Mortuary attendants and funeral home workers have been known to be caught sexually assaulting corpses, and there have been individuals who have dug up graves in order to obtain a dead body to have sex with. More commonly there are serial murderers such as Ed Gein, Ed Kemper, Jeffery Dahmer, and Garry Ridgeway who have taken sexual advantage of dead victims.'

What made this murder even worse was that the young son of Marilyn Peters was in the house at the time. Thankfully though, Little did not harm the child. William Little was most assuredly not a financially motivated killer because he left all the money and jewelry belonging to Peters that was in the house. He was arrested a few months after the murder. Little said he only knew Marilyn Peters vaguely because she sold him drugs from time to time. The police suspected that Little had been planning to rape Peters for some time. He had clearly decided in advance that he would kill her too.

The police found some old blood stains on Little's clothes which they were able to connect to the murder victim. As a consequence of this, Little's defence case was always pretty weak to say the least. Little claimed that he'd had consensual sex with Peters and then they'd argued and she attacked him. That was what you might describe as a preposterous whopper of a lie. His evidence was patently a string of desperate untruths.

For his harrowing and brutal murder of Marilyn Peters, William Little was sentenced to death. Little is one of the lesser known of the necrophilic killers who litter the history of true crime but had he not been caught it is probably safe to assume he would have committed more dark crimes of this nature and become much more famous. Thankfully, we never got to find this out for sure.

LAST MEAL?

There was a hearty but basic sort of last meal for William Little in 1999 before his execution. There was nothing too fancy on Little's last meal list - to the point where you half suspect he was merely given bumper portions of prison food rather than permitted to order anything too elaborate. Little had two pounds of bacon and three fried eggs to begin. He ate this with a generous amount of toast. He then had two burgers with cheese, onion, and tomato. Little had French fries and a salad dressing with his burger. For his dessert, Little simply had a big bowl of strawberries. To wash down this last supper he had some chocolate milk.

Strawberry Cheesecake

DANIEL LUCAS

CRIMES?

Daniel Anthony Lucas was sentenced to death for the 1998 killings of 37-year-old Steven Moss, his 11-year-old son Bryan and 15-year-old daughter Kristin, in central Georgia.
Lucas had been robbing the home of this family with an accomplice named Brandon Rhode. The son Bryan apparently noticed the men enter the house and tried to intervene. He was shot through the shoulder. He was then taken to a bedroom and shot several times. When the daughter got home from school she was also shot. The father Steven Moss got the same treatment whe he returned home.

Rhode is believed to have fired these initial bullets but then Lucas shot the victims several more times just to make certain they were dead. Lucas almost certainly shot people who were still alive. The duo had a shotgun so this was a messy crime scene. This evil duo then tried to drive off with the valuables they'd taken from the house but they were seen by neighbours. One of these neighbours was later able to ID Lucas as one of the suspicious men they'd seen leaving in the car.

The two men made a frantic attempt to get rid of the weapons they'd used for the murders but their efforts - thankfully - were to no avail and it didn't take long at all for them to be in custody. Friends of Rhode later told the cops that he'd told them he'd 'messed up' and killed some people. Lucas and Rhode were both sentenced to death for this awful home invasion robbery. Rhode was executed in 2010 but it took until 2016 for Lucas to be executed.

Daniel Lucas said he'd suffered from an abusive childhood and was also impaired by a brain injury he picked up as a child. Many killers, as we have noted, seem to have had head injuries of some sort. John Wayne Gacy is another notorious killer who suffered head injuries as a child. He was knocked out by a swing and once beaten senseless by his father. David Berkowitz (aka The Son of Sam) suffered a head injury at the age of six when he was struck by a car. Alexander Pichushkin (aka The Chessboard Killer) suffered a serious head injury as a child when he was in a playground. Dennis Rader said that when he was an infant his mother dropped him and he landed on his head.

Lucas confessed to the murder at first on videotape but later seemed to try and suggest he had been drunk at the time of his confession and had no idea what he'd been saying. The strategy of the defence team of Lucas was to argue that he was mentally impaired and dominated by the more assertive Rhode. While this may have had some element of truth the fact is though that Lucas was a full and active participant in this brutal and senseless slaying of an innocent family. The real sympathy resided with the mother of the children who discovered the bodies. She'd arrived home to find her husband and two children had all been shot dead.

Daniel Lucas spent half of his life on death row in the end

before he was executed. He apparently got into Buddhism while in prison. Sadly, it was all a bit late for that. It's a shame he didn't become a Buddhist before slaughtering that poor family. Lucas had Buddhist friends and family members visit him in his last days. They truly believed he was a changed man who was sorry for his crimes. Nonetheless, his execution went ahead as planned. He was 37 years-old.

LAST MEAL?

For his last meal, Lucas had a meat pizza. I always presumed Buddhists were vegetarian but maybe this isn't the case. Lucas also had a calzone. A calzone is an Italian oven-baked folded pizza. Lucas must be one of the few people on death row to order a calzone. It doesn't crop up very often in last meal requests. Daniel Lucas wasn't finished yet when it came to his last meal because he also had a steak, a salad, and a stuffed mushroom. Typical ingredients used for stuffed mushrooms are spinach, tomato, cheese, onion, garlic, meat, and herbs. Lucas washed his last supper down with orange juice. The prospect of being executed clearly hadn't done any harm to the appetite of Daniel Lucas because a friend later reported that prior to his last meal he'd indulged in honey buns and Cheetos from the prison vending machines.

RHONDA BELL MARTIN

CRIMES?

Rhonda Belle Martin was born in 1907. Martin was an Alabama waitress who confessed to poisoning to death several members of her family in 1956. She killed three daughters, her mother and two husbands, mostly with rat poison. Martin also attempted to kill her fifth husband (and former step-son) but he survived and was left a paraplegic.

The authorities were rather befuddled as to why she became a serial poisoner of relatives because the life insurance money and inheritances she accrued from these deaths was modest and barely covered all the funeral expenses. Rhonda Belle Martin never really offered an explanation as to why she had killed most of her family. It has been suggested that she became addicted to the attention and sympathy she received whenever a relative died.

Rhonda Belle Martin was rumbled when her latest husband survived his poisoning. An investigation soon deduced that many relatives of Martin had been poisoned. She used ant poison and arsenic to kill her relatives. The poison was often put in coffee and then served up to the victim. Rhonda Belle Martin was a rather unlikely serial killer as she was a plump and conservative looking bespectacled middle-aged housewife. Although she confessed to the murders her inability to explain why she had done them simply made her all the more baffling.

Martin's lawyer tried to go for a plea of insanity in court and suggest that Rhonda had (as you do!) bumped off her husband so she could marry her step-son. In the end she was only tried for the death of her fourth husband. That was more than sufficient to give her the harshest of sentences. It took a jury just over three hours to find her guilty. The sentence was death. Rhonda Belle Martin burst into tears at the verdict but was later quite stoic as her execution loomed.

LAST MEAL?

For her last meal, Rhonda Belle Martin had hamburger and mashed potatoes. This is such a plain last meal that one presumes it was simply the prison menu that day. Would anyone really choose mashed potato as their last meal on planet Earth? Martin also had a sweet cinnamon roll and some coffee. A cinnamon roll is a sweet roll commonly served in Northern Europe and North America. In Sweden it is called kanelbulle. All in all it was a rather prosaic and bland sort of last meal but maybe this was just the sort of food Rhonda Belle

TIMOTHY McVEIGH

Martin liked anyway.

TIMOTHY McVEIGH

CRIMES?

Timothy McVeigh was born in New York in 1968. McVeigh was a Gulf war veteran. In 1995 he detonated a truck bomb underneath a federal government building in Oklahoma City. 168 people died as a consequence and many more were badly injured. McVeigh is believed to have committed this terrorist act as 'revenge' for the 1993 Waco siege. McVeigh never expressed any regret or remorse for his crimes and said that given the chance he would do it again. McVeigh was a troubled young man who fallen down the crazy rabbit hole of conspiracies. He didn't seem unduly concerned by the death sentence handed to him either. McVeigh said he would rather die than spend his life in prison. His wish was granted. McVeigh was executed by lethal injection at 7:14 a.m. on June the 11th, 2001.

LAST MEAL?

There was nothing at all elaborate about Timothy McVeigh's last meal in the federal penitentiary in Terre Haute, Indiana. All he requested was two pints of mint chocolate chip ice cream. Mint chocolate chip is an ice cream flavor composed of mint ice cream with small chocolate chips. In some cases the liqueur crème de menthe is used to provide the mint flavor, but in most cases peppermint or spearmint flavouring is used. Food colouring is added to make it green. It has been alleged that mint chocolate chip ice cream was invented in 1973 by culinary student Marilyn Ricketts while studying at South Devon College in England. However, some American companies would probably claim that mint chocolate chip ice cream was used by them before this. Who knows what the real truth is? Trivia - mint chocolate chip is only the tenth most popular ice cream flavour.

PETER MINIEL

CRIMES?

On May the 8th, 1986, in Harris County, Texas, Peter Miniel and his friend, James Russell, Jr, murdered a twenty year-old man named Paul Manier in his apartment. The men were in the apartment to take drugs but when Paul Manier was distracted a beer glass was smashed over the back of his head. The unfortunate victim of this attack was then struck with a shock absorber and stabbed multiple times - thirty-nine in all. The knife was blunt so the stabbing was prolonged and brutal.

Miniel did the stabbing while Russell held the victim down. Miniel then slashed the victim's throat. Peter Miniel got a paltry haul for this murder. Just $20 that was in the victim's wallet and a stereo. It is believed that Miniel and Russell had gone to the apartment for a party but just before they went inside Miniel suggested that they rob Manier instead. This robbery quickly turned violent. It was so violent that the victim ended up with a hole in part of his skull.

Miniel and Russell cleaned themselves up after the murder and then went for a bite to eat in Burger King. Miniel couldn't have cared less that he'd just killed a person. He was more annoyed at their pathetic haul. $20 and a cheap stereo. It is presumed that Miniel had been hoping to find drugs in the house but to his dismay there were no drugs at all and no hidden stashes of cash or anything worth selling besides a modest stereo.

After the murder, Miniel fled to Indiana and then Chicago - where he was arrested a month later. Miniel confessed to the murder in the end and was sentenced to death by lethal injection. This was carried out in 2004. James Russell, Jr got a slightly lesser sentence of 50 years in prison (50 years in prison is not exactly a light sentence but it's probably better than being executed) by testifying against Miniel in court. Miniel had tried to blame the murder solely on Russell at one point but this wasn't very convincing. Both were to blame.

Peter Miniel said he was high and drunk at the time of the murder. Many killers say something like this. They seem to think it might somehow make a difference to their defence but it obviously doesn't. If you've murdered someone you are not going to get let off just because you'd had a few drinks at the time! Miniel was already known to the police before this murder and had a number of crimes on his slate. These included theft, disorderly conduct, and violent domestic abuse. He once attacked his girlfriend with a motorcycle chain and 'martial arts' weapons. It's safe to say that Peter Miniel was both highly disturbed and highly dangerous. He didn't show much emotion in court although before his execution he did offer an apology to the family of the victim.

LAST MEAL?

Peter Miniel's last meal must rank as one of the heartiest on record. He had two cheeseburgers to begin with. That's almost a meal in and of itself but Miniel wasn't finished yet. Oh no. He also had a load of beef tacos. A taco is a traditional Mexican food consisting of a small hand-sized corn or wheat-based tortilla topped with a filling. Miniel also had a generous amount of beef enchiladas. An enchilada is a corn tortilla rolled around a filling and covered with a sauce.

You would think that would be more than sufficient grub for a last meal but Miniel also had a pizza with jalapenos. He also requested fried chicken and spaghetti. There's surely no way he could have eaten all of this. You might presume that after that blowout there'd be no room for dessert but you'd be wrong about that. Miniel had three different types of cake (chocolate, vanilla, and fruit) with ice cream. The ice cream flavours he chose were cookies and cream and caramel pecan fudge. He washed this epic meal down with orange juice, Coca-Cola, root beer, and Pepsi. Miniel then retired to await his execution. I'd imagine his last request was probably Gaviscon.

JOHN GLENN MOODY

CRIMES?

John Glenn Moody was born in 1952. He was a habitual thief and criminal. In the mid 1980s he had three stints in prison for burglary, car theft, and assault. In all, he had nearly half a dozen criminal convictions and these included charges of sexual assault.

In 1987, in west Virginia, Moody - who was on parole at the time - killed 77 year-old Maureen Louise Maulden. He raped her and then strangled the victim to death with a telephone cord. Moody knew the victim because he had done some odd jobs at her house in the past. Maulden clearly trusted Moody - which turned out to be a big mistake. Maureen apparently had no idea about Moody's criminal history. It's probably safe to presume that Moody kept his thieving and prison stints out of his CV when he was trying to pick up some casual work.

It was Maureen's sister who found the body. Maureen's son was so traumatised by this terrible murder that he took his own life a few years later. It was obviously devastating for the family. Maureen Louise Maulden was by all accounts a kind and generous woman and a pillar of the local community. She didn't deserve what happened to her. Police officers who worked on this case said it was one of the worst they had experienced. Maureen had been beaten to a pulp by a fireplace poker before her death.

Thankfully, John Glenn Moody did not prove to be the most elusive of murderers. He was arrested for public drunkenness not long after and the cops got suspicious when they heard that he'd told his wife to dispose of some 'hot' rings during a prison visit. The rings belonged to Maureen Louise Maulden. The key piece of evidence was the police finding a bloodied fingerprint on Maureen's telephone. Both the blood and the fingerprint matched Moody. That was basically case closed.

Moody was found guilty of capital murder and sentenced to death. There was a lot of soul-searching about this murder because it appeared that the criminal system had failed Maureen Louise Maulden. Given his lengthy raft of crimes, should Moody have even been on parole in the first place? John Glenn Moody's defence was hindered by the fact that he kept changing his story. He could never really decide which lie he was going to stick with and so kept changing his evidence. This merely made him an unreliable narrator. Not that it mattered anyway. The forensic evidence was more than sufficient.

Moody was eventually executed by lethal injection in 1999. He had maintained his innocence for much of his prison stretch but did offer an apology to Maureen's family before the execution. Not that it was much of a consolation to them. Moody had shown no remorse during the trial so it was probably a bit late for that now.

LAST MEAL?

For his last meal, John Glenn Moody went for two T-bone steaks with French fries. He had some bread rolls with this main course and also a salad with French dressing. He also had five tacos. Moody had an Angel cake for dessert. Angel cake is basically a sponge cake. Angel cake is actually healthier than normal cake because it doesn't contain butter or egg yolks. The cake is often served with strawberries and cream. Moody eschewed this though and had chocolate almond ice cream with his cake. To wash down this food, Moody had a six pack of Pepsi cola.

BENITO MUSSOLINI

CRIMES?

Benito Mussolini (1883–1945) was the dictator of Italy for most of the war. Italy joined Nazi Germany and Japan to become known as the Axis Powers. He ruled Italy from 1922 until he was deposed in 1943. He later became the leader of the Italian Social Republic (a Nazi puppet regime in the north of Italy) after he was rescued by German special forces. Mussolini moved fast to create a totalitarian state in the early days and managed to gain complete control of the country.

Known as Il Duce ("the leader"), Mussolini was pompous and arrogant and the poor performance of the Italian armed forces in World War 2 never gave him an especially strong hand to play in his meetings with Hitler. Mussolini threw Italy behind Hitler's Germany in the war as he was sure that the Nazis would dominate Europe and successfully invade Great Britain. Mussolini had a particular dislike of Britain and wanted the Royal Navy's dominance of the Mediterranean ended. Although the Italian Army was nowhere near as modern, formidable, powerful and professional as the German one, Mussolini believed that they had to show a willingness to fight and make sacrifices to get a jackal's share of the bounty in the new Nazi Europe that was coming.

Unfortunately for Mussolini this led to no small degree of humiliation when the Italian campaigns in Greece and North Africa were unsuccessful and Hitler had to dispatch German troops to help them. In October 1940, Mussolini invaded Greece from Albania. He had assumed Greece would be easy pickings but his army was driven back into Albania by the Greeks. It was, to say the least, very humiliating for Mussolini.

Mussolini hadn't bothered to tell Hitler about his invasion of Greece. Hitler was furious when he found out. The Germans had to intervene to help Italy and also prevent the British from occupying Greece first. Mussolini is believed to have invaded Greece in a fit of pique because he was angry that Hitler had annexed Romania without consulting Italy. Italy considered Romania to be part of their sphere of influence.

The eventual Axis collapse in North Africa had profound consequences for Italy because it meant they were the next target for the Allies. Mussolini had also committed an Italian army of 235,000 soldiers to fight alongside the Germans in the Soviet Union but the army was eventually destroyed there with only the remnants returning home. The Italian and Romanian soldiers on the eastern front were what you might call reluctant allies. They had antiquated equipment and no great appetite for battle.

The Soviets often targeted the areas held by the Italian and Romanian divisions because these formations were much weaker than the German divisions. The Italian army in the Soviet Union was destroyed by the defeat at Stalingrad. Over 80,000 were killed or captured and those that did return home were shattered both mentally and physically from their grim experiences. Italian veterans who survived the eastern front said that their weapons were unreliable and useless and that the Italian Army was poorly trained and equipped. They blamed Mussolini for sacrificing them just so that he could keep in favour with Hitler.

With Italy tired of war and military disasters and aware that the Axis now looked like the losing side, Mussolini was deposed by King Victor Emmanuel III in 1943 but rescued by Otto Skorzeny on the orders of Hitler and smuggled to Germany. The war had gone sour for Italy and everyone was aware the Allies were on the way to victory. Italy was more or less a puppet state run by Germany and Mussolini was bitter and frustrated.

He wrote his memoirs and tried to shift the blame for the disasters and humiliations heaped upon the Italian armed forces in the war onto others. After the German collapse, Mussolini tried to escape across the Swiss border in April 1945. Mussolini, his mistress Clara Petacci, and fascist leaders, were captured by Italian partisans. They were shot and then the bodies of Mussolini and Petacci were dumped on the Piazzale Loreta, a suburban square near the main railway station. This spot was chosen because fifteen partisans had been executed there in 1944. A crowd soon gathered and the bodies of Mussolini and his mistress were beaten and spat at. The bodies were then hung up on public display at a petrol station. When Hitler heard of this it strengthened his resolve not to be captured alive.

LAST MEAL?

We don't know what Mussolini had for his last meal but we do know a fair bit about his diet. Mussolini suffered from a stomach ulcer and had an eccentric diet. He only ate rice, eggs, boiled onions, a small amount of meat, and a lot of fruit. One visitor later said Mussolini ate seven pounds of grapes a day and only drank milk. Mussolini would often eat a salad consisting of only garlic and lemon juice. He believed garlic was good for his heart so did his best to eat a lot of it. One imagines his breath wasn't too pleasant after indulging in this salad.

Mussolini was sort of like the Putin of his day in that he was often pictured shirtless or on horseback or doing some exercise. He tried to play the role of the energetic virile strong man. In reality though Mussolini hated exercise and was never especially fit. One can see evidence of this in his stocky frame. He was clearly carrying a few too many pounds. Despite being Italian, Mussolini didn't like pasta because he thought it made you sluggish. He was a fan of olive oil though. Mussolini was said to have a particular disdain for French food - which he described as 'useless'.

DENNIS NILSEN

CRIMES?

Dennis Andrew Nilsen was born in 1945 in Fraserburgh, Aberdeenshire, Scotland. Nilsen is one of the worst serial killers in British history. Nilsen eventually confessed to murdering fifteen men and said he tried to kill others. His spree took place from 1978 to 1983. Dennis Nilsen's confirmed verified victims are Kenneth Ockenden, Martyn Duffey, William Sutherland, Stephen Holmes, Malcolm Barlow, John Howlett and Stephen Sinclair. The victims were usually gay men of no fixed abode. He would often strangle the victims while they were asleep and sometimes drowned them in the bath. Dennis Nilsen's motive for murder was almost identical to Jeffrey Dahmer. Both of these notorious figures said that they killed because they didn't want the men they had met to leave them. They both, in their warped way, decided that being with a dead person was better than being alone.
Nilsen admitted that he used to talk to the corpses of his victims as if they were alive.

As a young man, Nilsen became obsessed with a painting called The Raft of the Medusa by the French Romantic painter and lithographer Théodore Géricault. The painting depicts the French naval ship Méduse as it arrived in Mauritania on July 5, 1816 after experiencing problems on it's journey leading to get damage to the Meduse as well as large numbers of casualties in the crew. What made Nilsen so disturbing was the way he came across as completely calm and highly articulate and thoughtful in interviews. If you met him you would have no idea that he was so dangerous. While many serial killers are reluctant to speak about their crimes or (ludicrously) maintain their innocence, Dennis Nilsen loved to talk about his murders and would discuss them for hours if given the chance. He seemed to crave attention.
Nilsen grew up in a small fishing port. He said it was a lonely

existence. Nilsen had an obsession (a fetish one might say) with death. He saw a beautiful serenity and peace in death. This stemmed from a childhood experience when he saw his dead maternal grandfather Andrew Whyte. Nilsen said that looking at dead people also made him feel invulnerable. As a young man, Dennis Nilsen would smear himself with white makeup and talcum powder and pretend he was dead. He said he found this erotic. Nilsen deduced that he was gay at a young age. He said that this created a feeling of tension and alienation because he grew up at a time when being gay was still actually against the law.

Dennis Nilsen joined the Army Cadet Force when he was fourteen. He then served in the British Army Catering Corps and was a chef in 1st Battalion the Royal Fusiliers. Nilsen was stationed in Aldershot, Norway, Germany, Plymouth, the Shetland Islands, and the Middle East during his army career. Nilsen served eleven years in the army and reached the rank of corporal. It was in the army that Dennis Nilsen learned how to butcher meat. He would use this skill on his dead victims when he became a serial killer. In 1972, Dennis Nilsen moved to London to join the police. He completed his police training course and passed his exams. Nilsen had been posted to Wilsden Green Police Station and served as a beat bobby before he decided that this wasn't the career for him. When he was in the police, Dennis Nilsen had to view autopsied bodies in the morgue. He found this experience completely fascinating and sexually exciting.

Dennis Nilsen became a civil servant after he dropped out of the police. He was a recruitment interviewer. Nilsen, at the time of his arrest, was the Acting Executive Officer at the employment office on Denmark Street, Soho. In 1975, Dennis Nilsen began a relationship with a man named David Gallichan. They moved in together at Melrose Avenue and were happy at first. However, when Gallichan eventually decided to leave, this left Nilsen feeling lonely and abandoned. Nilsen claimed that he ordered Gallichan to leave. Whatever the truth, the fact that Nilsen was left all alone was devastating

for his already fragile mental health. Old home movies of
Dennis Nilsen and David Gallichan together suggest that
Nilsen was the dominant personality in the relationship. One
can see in them that Nilsen is an irritable man who likes to be
in control of a situation. Nilsen always seems to be in a bad
mood in these amateur films. Nilsen murdered someone for
the first time eighteen months after David Gallichan moved
out of the flat they shared.

Dennis Nilsen's first victim was Stephen Holmes. Stephen
went missing in December 1978 and was only fourteen years-
old. Stephen Holmes spent the night with Dennis Nilsen.
Nilsen didn't want Stephen Holmes to leave and so strangled
and drowned him. He washed the body (including the hair)
and abused the corpse sexually. Dennis Nilsen's passion for
necrophilia was the main motive for his murders. Nilsen said
he was amazed to discover how easy it was to kill someone
without anyone noticing. After he killed for the first time,
Nilsen purchased an electric knife to dismember the victim but
couldn't go through with it. He then began to see the beauty
(from his point of view) in a dead body and decided to wash
and keep the corpse. Dennis Nilsen would put plastic sheets or
bin-liners on the floor before he dissected his victims. He said
he would vomit in the sink a few times while he did this grisly
task. Dennis Nilsen's murders are felt to have been spur of the
moment because of his great difficulties in disposing of
evidence. There wasn't much sign of any planning or thought
about them.

When he lived at 195 Melrose Avenue, Dennis Nilsen had
access to a garden out the back. He was able to dispose of
some of victims by burning them on a bonfire. Nilsen had to
throw some tyres onto the bonfire to mask the odour of
burning flesh and organs. However, this never alerted any
suspicion. One could hardly blame the neighbours. If you see
someone having a bonfire the last thing you assume is that
they are burning a dead body! Dennis Nilsen had to leave 195
Melrose Avenue because the landlord wanted to renovate the
flat. When he moved to Cranley Gardens, Nilsen no longer had

access to a garden and so disposing of the bodies became much more difficult. When he lived at 195 Melrose Avenue, Dennis Nilsen was a victim of burglers and two detectives came to the flat. Nilsen was amazed that the detectives didn't notice the foul odour seeped into his home from all the body parts.

Dennis Nilsen used a ligature to strangle his victims. Often it was a necktie. There were a few incidents of neighbours complaining of a smell coming from Nilsen's 195 Melrose Avenue flat. Nilsen told them that the odour stemmed from structural problems in the building. Nilsen sometimes put the torsos of victims in suitcases until he had a chance to burn them. The big cooking pot that Nilsen used to boil skulls, hands, and feet, was brought to his trial to be used as evidence. Dennis Nilsen's last flat was in a very grotty and squalid condition when he was arrested. It was absolutely filthy with plates and empty food containers piled up. The oven was covered in dirt and everything was old, tattered, rusted, and falling apart.

One of Dennis Nilsen's victims was a young man named Malcolm Barlow. Barlow suffered from epilepsy and had been found by Nilsen in the street looking unwell. Nilsen got him an ambulance and they parted. Tragically though, Barlow returned to Nilsen's building the next day and waited for him to get home from work. Nilsen found Barlow's presence an irritation and so he killed him. Graham Allen was Nilsen's second to last victim. Nilsen kept Allen's body in his bath for several days after he killed him. Nilsen would boil the heads of his victims and then pick off the flesh so he could try and flush it down the toilet.

Dennis Nilsen was captured because a plumbing company was called out to unblock the drain outside his building. Nilsen had been trying to flush body parts and bones down the toilet. Tests on the bones and remains blocking the drain found that they were human and the drainpipe led directly to Nilsen's flat. When the police searched Nilsen's flat they encountered a nightmarish scene. Nielsen had body parts and torsos hidden all over the place. He even had bags containing the heads of some of his victims. After he was arrested, Nielsen said to a police psychiatrist of his victims that - "They would sit down. I would talk incessantly like an auctioneer. Outpourings about music, politics, Margaret Thatcher etc. All completely cynical. If they entered into it, they would be OK. If they were sleeping, they would be dead already. It was the ultimate reply to apathy." This was a rather chilling statement because it implied that Nilsen would kill people who mildly irritated him.

Denis Nilsen wrote of his crimes - 'I did it all for me. Purely selfish. I worshiped the art and the act of death, over and over. It's as simple as that. Afterwards it was all sexual confusion, symbolism, honoring the "fallen." I was honoring myself. I hated the decay and the dissection. There was no sadistic pleasure in the killing. I killed them as I would like to be killed myself, enjoying the extremity of the death act itself. If I did it to myself I could only experience it once. If I did it to others, I could experience the death act over and over again.' Nilsen was sentenced to life imprisonment with a recommendation that he serve a minimum of 25 years.

Many felt that the Dennis Nilsen trial indicated that definitions of sanity and diminished responsibility needed to be looked at again. While it was true that Nilsen was aware of what he had done and seemed 'normal' in person it would be ludicrous all the same to call him sane given his crimes. This was a man who could make a cup of tea at the same time as he was boiling a human head on another hob ring. Nilsen was genuinely odd in that he wasn't insane but, all the same, didn't seem to comprehend that he had done grotesque and harrowing things. This is a man who would sit watching television with a corpse next to him.

Nilsen was moved around a number of prisons and even fought a (obviously doomed) battle to release an autobiography and music albums. Nilsen wrote tens of thousands of words in an attempt to self diagnose himself. The condensed version is that he was a misfit who found dead bodies attractive. Nilsen was interviewed for television once in prison but the interview only amounted to a few minutes as part of a documentary. In the interview Nilsen said that congealed blood made dissecting bodies less messy than it might appear. It seemed to be a source of irritation to Nilsen that he couldn't be interviewed more. His ego and vanity would have enjoyed more chances to appear to TV.

Dennis Nilsen killed all those men because he knew the connection he had with them was fleeting. He knew they would leave him and he didn't want that to happen. Nilsen once wrote - 'I had always held within me a fear of emotional rejection and failure. Nobody ever really got close to me. There was never a place for me in the scheme of things. My inner emotions could not be expressed, and this led me to the alternative of a retrograde and deepening imagination. I had become a living fantasy on a theme in dark endless dirges.' Nilsen's inability to cope with rejection became fused with a lifelong yearning for necrophilia. If he killed these men then they would never be able to leave him and he would also have complete control over them.

Nilsen could fufil his two greatest fantasies through murder. Until such time as decomposition took place that is. When this happened, Nilsen's necrophilia fantasies evaporated and gave way to more traditional serial killer headaches like having to get rid of bodies and body parts. You might suggest loneliness made Nilsen do these terrible things but that barely feels like a satisfactory answer. Most people feel lonely at times but they don't become Dennis Nilsen as a consequence. The most salient actor in Nilsen's crimes was necrophilia. Nilsen was addicted to the power he felt when he had mastery of a dead person. He was acting out his darkest fantasy. The fantasy could never be permanent though. The bodies would inevitably decay and smell. They had to be disposed of. Nilsen then had to kill again to begin the fantasy afresh. It was what you might describe as a classic example of a vicious circle. Dennis Nilsen died in prison in 2018 at the age of 72. He was truly one of the most disturbing British serial killers of all time. He tends to be known as The Company Killer now because he never wanted his victims to leave him.

LAST MEAL?

We don't know what the last thing Dennis Nilsen ate was but we do know a lot about his food habits and cooking history. Dennis Nilsen was said to make a great curry and be an expert at whipping up omlettes. When he was in the army, he once cooked for the detainees at Al Masousa gaol in Aden - which was ironic in light of his later life. Dennis Nilsen was selected to cook for the Queen's Royal Guard in 1971. This never happened though because he was posted elsewhere. Nilsen's regiment took part though in a parade in front of the Queen and Field Marshal Montgomery. Dennis Nilsen's mother said that when he visited home during his time in the army he was always proud to display his new cooking skills.

In 1979, the Jobcentre he worked at had a big Christmas party that Dennis Nilsen helped to organise. Nilsen brought in some pots and pans and cooked for eighty people. It is of course rather harrowing to think of what those pots and pans might have been used for in Nilsen's flat. Nilsen cooked in the army 'galley' style and gave his cooking skills a rare display. Dennis Nilsen also liked to make mulled wine for his work colleagues at Christmas.

Despite his fabled army cooking skills, those who visited Dennis Nilsen said that he very rarely had any food in the cupboard or his fridge. David Gallichan said that Nilsen never cooked and got by on cheap takeaways. Despite his time as a cook, Nilsen was a man of simple tastes when it came to food. He liked takeaways, fried eggs, and crisps - which obviously wasn't what you would call health food. Those that knew Dennis Nilsen said it was hard to believe he was a trained chef because he hardly ever used his oven. Nilsen didn't care if he had to get by on a piece of toast for his dinner. He seemed to have little interest in food. It appears as if eleven years in the

Army Catering Corps had put Nilsen off cooking for life. He simply couldn't be bothered with it. You probably won't be surprised to hear that there are no instances of Nilsen ever hosting a dinner party.

Nilsen always looked lean and fit but this was misleading. He had smoked since he was fourteen and was a heavy drinker. Dennis Nilsen's favourite rum was Captain Morgan's Black Label. Dennis Nilsen and Jeffrey Dahmer both had the same favourite tipple. They were both partial to rum & coke. Dennis Nilsen was also said to drink a lot of Bacardi and Coke. Those who visited Dennis Nilsen say that he was quite fond of whiskey too. Nilsen drank lager now and again but he preferred spirits. Nilsen liked to get drunk as fast as possible.

After his death, Dennis Nilsen's spectacles were given to a woman named Andrea Kubinova in the Czech Republic. Kubinova was Nilsen's penpal and visited him in prison. "He came across as a nice person," she said. "I know it's odd in the context, but yeah he was." Andrea Kubinova said that Dennis Nilsen told her he had no visitors in prison and that his surviving family had all disowned him. Andrea Kubinova said that when she met Dennis Nilsen in prison he was unrecognisable from the Dennis Nilsen of 1983. His hair was white and he was a rather hunched and frail figure.

Kubinova said that Dennis Nilsen had a great love of cheese & onion crisps and was fond of using the Oscar Wilde quote - 'The only worse than being talked about is NOT being talked about. In letters to Andrea Kubinova from prison, Dennis Nilsen said that he loved to watch Dad's Army. He described it as perfect comfort television. Andrea Kubinova said that Dennis Nilsen told her that his favourite food in prison was a fried egg sandwich. Andrea Kubinova also said that Dennis Nilsen told her that he dried his washing in prison on the radiator pipes. The letters painted a picture of a lonely old man living a tedious life behind bars.

Salad

MARION ALBERT PRUETT

CRIMES?

Marion Albert Pruett was born in North Carolina in 1949. Pruett was a robber and serial killer although his case is rather unusual in that he was once in witness protection for information he divulged about a prison killing. It later transpired that Pruett may well have been responsible himself for the prison slaying in question. He was a nutty looking character with big bulging eyes. This quality was heightened by the fact that he wore spectacles.

Pruett used his assumed identity in the witness protection scheme to his advantage by committing a host of crimes under his new false persona. He is believed to have killed at least five people. Most of the victims were store clerks who were unlucky enough to be on duty at the stores this maniac was robbing. Pruett was a very sadistic man. He is believed to have beaten his common-law-wife to death with a hammer and then set her on fire. Pruett said he robbed and killed to support his cocaine habit. He was a very dangerous and violent criminal.

Thankfully, the law finally caught up with this ghastly man in 1982 and he was taken into custody. He was executed by lethal injection in April, 1999. When he was on death row, Pruett tried to obtain money from the media for disclosing the whereabouts of victims and their remains. One of his requests was to appear on a television talk show. None of these requests were obviously granted. Pruett was one of those killers who enjoyed his notoriety and seemed to think he was now a celebrity. His ego would doubtless have been dented though by the fact that there was relatively little media coverage of his trial. You might describe Pruett as a 'forgotten' serial killer. He simply wasn't that well known compared to some other killers of his era.

LAST MEAL?

Marion Albert Pruett certainly didn't hold back when it came to his last meal. He went for a shuddering table creaker of epic proportions. When you have an imminent date with a lethal injection those diet plans tend to go right out of the window. Pruett began his feast with a stuffed crust pizza from Pizza Hut. This pizza, as fast food fans will be well aware, has string cheese in the crust. Pruett then had no less than four Burger King Whoppers. One would think you'd be pretty stuffed after a pizza and four burgers but Marion Albert Pruett was far from finished.

He also had some fried eggplant (aubergine), fried squash, and fried okra. Okra is a plant in the mallow family. Marion Albert Pruett couldn't be accused of not eating his vegetables - although he rather negated the health benefits by having them fried to within an inch of their lives. To wash this meal down he had three bottles of Pepsi. Oh, I forgot to mention that he had an order of French fries too.

For his pudding this deadly killer had some pecan pie. Pecan pie is a pie of pecan nuts mixed with a filling of eggs, butter, and sugar. Variations may include white or brown sugar, cane syrup, sugar syrup, molasses, maple syrup, or honey. Strange but true - Marion Albert Pruett's original last meal request was actually roast duck but the prison kitchen declined to procure and cook one for him.

RICKY RAY RECTOR

CRIMES?

Ricky Ray Rector was born in 1950. He was convicted for two counts of murder (which happened in 1981) and sentenced to death in Arkansas. Not much is known about Rector's past. In 1981 he went beserk at a diner and pulled out a gun. One man was shot and another injured. Rector became a fugitive for a few days but was persuaded by his mother to turn himself in. Rector agreed to do this but stipulated that he would only turn himself in to a local police officer named Robert Martin he had known since he was a child. This was arranged but Rector then shot the unfortunate police officer dead before turning the gun on himself.

Rector survived his attempted suicide but was left with frontal lobe damage. He was essentially now brain damaged and not the man he used to be. His defence team argued, with some justification, that this made him mentally impaired and unfit for a trial. They felt Rector should now be confined to life in some sort of institution or hospital. That would be the humane and human thing to do in this awful case.

These logical arguments all counted for nothing in the end though and Rector was tried and sentenced to death. Rector was eventually executed by lethal injection in 1992. It took fifty minutes to find a vein for the injection and so Rector suffered greatly before his death. The governor of Arkansas at the time, a certain Bill Clinton, actually cut short his election campaigning to reaffirm that - despite protests - Rector would be executed. This was seen as very cynical and heartless to say the least. Clinton was absolutely shameless in the way he used Rector's death for political gain.

Clinton was desperate to be seen as tough on crime and the fate of a mentally impaired man was clearly very secondary to his desire to win a few extra votes. In 2002 the U.S Supreme Court banned the executions of those with mental impairments. Clinton had no such qualms though back in 1992. He couldn't have cared less. Rector was so mentally incompetent that when he had his last meal he asked for some of his dessert to be saved so he could eat it later. He evidently had no idea that that he was about to be executed.

LAST MEAL?

For his last ever meal, Ricky Ray Rector kept it fairly simple and had a steak and some fried chicken. This was clearly more than sufficient for him and so there were no French fries or side dishes. Rector also had some pecan pie. Pecan pie seems to be quite popular on death row. Rector's choice of beverage was cherry Kool-Aid. Kool-Aid is an American brand of flavored drink mix owned by Kraft Heinz based in Chicago, Illinois. The powder form was created by Edwin Perkins in 1927 based upon a liquid concentrate called Fruit Smack. You can buy Kool-Aid online outside the United States. It's a fizzy drink which you mix from a sachet.

The phrase 'drinking the Kool-Aid' has entered the lexicon of American culture thanks to the 1978 Jonestown Massacre where the cult followers of Jim Jones committed suicide in Guyana. They are alleged to have drunk poisoned Kool-Aid although many contend this is an urban myth and they actually used another soft drink. Anyway, to this day, anyone who is deemed to be gullible or dangerously misguided is still sometimes accused of 'drinking the Kool-Aid'.

PAUL EZRA RHOADES

CRIMES?

Paul Ezra Rhoades was born in Idaho in 1967. He tends to be classified as a spree killer and his official murder tally is listed as three. However, he has been linked to several other murders and if this was ever verified that obviously would classify him as a serial killer. Rhoades was a thief and drug addict from a young age. His crimes escalated in gravity as he got older. He appears to be one of those people who was always destined for trouble. Paul Ezra Rhoades was simply bad news.

His (official) crimes occurred over the span of a month early in 1987. Rhoades shot 21-year-old Stacy Dawn Baldwin, 20-year-old Nolan Haddon, and 34-year-old Susan Michelbacher. Baldwin and Haddon were store clerks killed in robberies. Baldwin was shot three times in a robbery which turned violent. Haddon was also shot. She survived for a time but then died in hospital. Michelbacher was a teacher who Rhoades abducted near a supermarket. She was raped and then shot nine times by Rhoades.

This last death was especially grim because there is evidence that Rhoades had sex with the body after the murder. Necrophilia is not uncommon amongst the most notorious serial killers. Ownership and total control of a person is a common fantasy that fuels the depraved activities of the worst serial killers. It is a popular thread with many serial killers that their sexual fantasies from a young age were about people who are restrained or can't move or struggle.

Social scientists say that the desire for control and dominance we see in serial killers often stems from an unhappy childhood where they felt weak and vulnerable. Many serial killers love the thought of having a helpless sexual victim at their mercy and you don't get more helpless than being dead. A study once found that 86% of serial killers had violent sexual fantasies that involved mutilation and restrained victims.

There had to be separate trials for these murders. The defence team of Rhoades argued that the evidence against him was circumstantial and that he had an alibi for one of the murders because he was babysitting for a relative at the time. The prosecution argued though that the bullets found in the victims matched Rhoades' gun and that shoeprints from him had been found in the stores where the murders took place. When he was found guilty in court, Paul Ezra Rhoades tried to throw a chair at the prosecutor. Someone managed to catch this flying chair though before it did any damage.

Paul Ezra Rhoades was executed by lethal injection in Idaho in 2011. He eventually confessed to the killing of Susan Michelbacher but denied involvement in the other murders. It's probably safe to say that no one believed him. His legal team filed many appeals to stave off his execution but eventually ran out of time and options.

LAST MEAL?

Paul Ezra Rhoades apparently didn't get to choose a special meal and so just had something that was on the prison menu that day. Rhoades had hot dogs with sauerkraut, mustard, ketchup, onions, relish, ranch dressing, and baked beans. It's strange that no death row prisoners never seem to choose hot dogs. They nearly always go for burgers. You'd think hot dogs would be more popular wouldn't you?

Rhoades also had some veggie chips. Vegetable chips are chips that are prepared using vegetables other than potatoes. Vegetable chips may be fried, deep-fried, dehydrated, dried or baked. For his dessert, Rhoades had fruit with gelatin and strawberry ice cream cups. As befitting a prison menu meal, it was a fairly standard and basic sort of last feast.

DANNY ROLLING

CRIMES?

Danny Harold Rolling was born in 1954 in Shreveport, Louisiana. Rolling, who became known as The Gainsville Ripper, was one of the inspirations for the Wes Craven movie Scream. Rolling had a habit of stalking and killing students. Rolling had a very unhappy childhood. His father, who was a policeman, was incredibly strict and abusive. He is said to hit Rolling while he was still a baby for not learning how to walk yet. That's how strict he was. Rolling's mother was so unhappy in her marriage to this demanding man that she tried to slash her own wrists. Rolling wasn't much of a student and failed all of his classes in school. He displayed early signs of being a peeping Tom and apparently discovered alcohol and drugs at a young age.

Rolling had a number of stints in prison for theft and his stock in trade became armed robbery. He escaped from prison a few times but always seemed to end back inside. Outside of prison, Rolling was practically unemployable by now. He was a habitual criminal who had virtually given up on 'straight' life. In 1990, Danny Rolling shot his father twice. His father survived the attack but lost an eye. By now, Danny Rolling had been in and out of prison a few times for theft. After he shot his father, Rolling fled and made his way to Florida where he used a fake ID to hide his real name. Rolling was now calling himself Michael Kennedy Jr.

Danny Rolling's worst crimes took place when he moved to Florida. In 1990 he forced his way into the home of two University of Florida students and raped and killed them. He abused the victims sexually when they were dead and cut off one of the student's nipples. The next day he forced his way into the apartment of another teenager and raped and killed her. He decapitated the victim and left the head next to some books. Rolling then killed two more students in the same month in equally grisly fashion. One was murdered in her bed.

Danny Rolling was living in some woods near the University of Florida as a homeless person at the time of his student attacks. This explained why he seemed to have such easy and quick access to the campus. Rolling carried cleaning fluids around with him so that he could clean up his crime scenes and negate the possibility of leaving DNA. He liked to leave his victims in suggestive sexual poses. The sense of terror on the Florida campus at this time was, as you can imagine, considerable. Many female students quickly packed their bags and left the university - never to return. You can hardly blame them.

All of the victims were brunettes with brown eyes - which suggested that Rolling had a specific preference for what type of victim he wanted. Danny Rolling was thankfully captured soon after his attacks on the students in Florida. He was arrested for robbery and the police noticed that the tools he possessed seemed to match the evidence of tools used in the University of Florida attacks. A DNA test managed to obtain a match between Rolling's DNA and some DNA found at the scene of the murders (Rolling was obviously not quite as thorough as he thought when it came to cleaning up crime scenes).

Rolling had a bag which contained a screwdriver, duct tape, a knife, and a gun. These were his grisly tools of the trade. Once he was in custody he confessed to the murders of the students. Rolling was then linked to the murder of a family in Shreveport that happened in 1989. In these murders, the victims and crime scene had been cleaned with cleaning agents and the youngest female had been positioned in a sexual pose after death. This matched the modus operandi of Danny Rolling. Rolling was sentenced to death on April the 20th, 1994. He was executed by lethal injection at Florida State Prison on October the 25th, 2006.

LAST MEAL?

Danny Rolling was another death row inmate with a fondness for seafood. He eschewed the usual pizza and burgers and went for lobster tail and butterfly shrimp. As a side dish he had a baked potato. What is it with death row inmates and baked potatoes? You honestly wouldn't think baked potatoes would be so popular when it comes to last meals.

As far as death row meals go, Rolling's was quite sophisticated and healthy. He even eschewed that old staple Coca-Cola and washed his last supper down with sweet tea. Sweet tea is a drink popular in the south of the United States. It is made by adding sugar or syrup to tea and is usually served cold. Lemon and ice is sometimes added. For his dessert, Rolling requested strawberry cheesecake rather than ice cream. Cheesecake is delicious and a pretty old dessert as it originated in ancient Greece. Danny Rolling's last meal was quite light by death row standards.

JOHN MARTIN SCRIPPS

CRIMES?

John Martin Scripps was born in Letchworth, Hertfordshire, 1959. John Martin Scripps was an Englishman who murdered three tourists in Singapore and Thailand. British tabloids called him (with good reason) The Tourist From Hell. Scripps used butchery knives to dismember his victims. He was executed in Singapore in 1996. This made him only the second westerner to be given the death sentence in Singapore since the country became independent from Britain.

Like many killers, Scripps was a thief and petty criminal before he resorted to murder. His first criminal conviction was for theft in 1974. He also earned a conviction for indecent assault.

Scripps went to Mexico to travel in 1980 and also got married. His marriage didn't last though. He became a drug trafficker in the end and travelled extensively. In 1987 he was caught in possession of drugs at Heathrow Airport and eventually received seven years in prison. Towards the end of his sentence Scripps, who was by all accounts a model prisoner, was given a transfer to a Category C prison. This is a prison with less lax security because those there are deemed unlikely to attempt escape. Guess what? Scripps DID escape - presumably because he was frustrated by his lack of parole. He was aided by his mother - who gave him some money to flee abroad.

Using a fake identity, Scripps fled prison and went back to Mexico. Scripp's murders later took place in Singapore and Thailand. He would pose as a tourist and strike up a conversation with someone. His first victim was a South African named Gerard Lowe in Singapore in 1995. Lowe was in the country as a tourist to shop and he got friendly with Scripps - agreeing they should share a hotel room to save money. This turned out to be a big mistake.

Scripps would incapacitate his victims with an electrical weapon and then strike them with a hammer. Scripps had learned butchery skills while in a British prison and so would use these skills to dismember his victims. Scripps chopped up Gerald Lowe and dumped the different parts of him in separate areas in plastic bags. Scripps was also savvy enough to somehow persuade a hotel receptionist to scrub Lowe's name from the guest register - though in the end it was still deduced that Lowe had been there.

Sheila and Darin Damude were a mother and son from Canada who Scripps then got friendly with because they had fairly adjacent hotel rooms in Thailand. When the mother and son didn't turn up for breakfast, Scripps told the receptionist they had checked out and that he would settle their bill. The skulls of Sheila and Darin Damude were later found at a tin mine. Scripps had murdered them both. Scripps was going by the name of Simon Davis and the local police became suspicious when they managed to deduce that Gerald Lowe had checked into a hotel with someone of that name.

When the police apprehended Scripps they found him in possession of various forged passports and credit cards belonging to his victims. Scripps also had an extensive 'murder kit' that included mace, an electroshock weapon, thumbcuffs, a hammer, and various knives. Scripps was charged with theft, forgery, and - of course - murder (for the death of Gerald Lowe). At his trial, Scripps claimed he had killed Lowe in self-defence because he had woken up and found Lowe sexually assaulting him. This defence was not very convincing. He said a friend had helped him dispose of the body but refused to elaborate on who this friend was.

You probably won't be surprised to hear that Scripps also denied murdering the Damudes. The prosecution however proved otherwise. They established there was clear connection in the methods of murder and disposal of Lowe and the Damudes which suggested the same killer was responsible. The fact that Scripps had encountered all the victims in hotels before their deaths was no coincidence. John Martin Scripps was sentenced to death by hanging.

Four days before his appeal was due to heard, Scripps dropped his appeal altogether. No one is quite sure why he did this. Perhaps he thought it was doomed to failure anyway. Maybe he was fed up with grim prison conditions and welcomed death? A clearly disinterested British Foreign Office did not submit a plea for clemency to Singapore and generally couldn't have cared less about the fate of Scripps. This was rather odd as British governments are supposed to be very anti-death penalty.

LAST MEAL?

John Martin Scripps kept it fairly simple when it came to his last meal. He went for a classic comfort food and drink combination. All he asked for was a pizza and some hot chocolate. The first chocolate drink is believed to have been created by the Maya around 2,500–3,000 years ago. Who doesn't love a mug of hot chocolate? It's the perfect drink for winter months. Hot chocolate can be made with water or milk but it is nicer with milk. It seems to be traditional in the United States to put marshmallows on top of the hot chocolate.

As ever with serial killers (though Scripps was arguably more of a spree killer), Scripps is suspected of killing more than his official victim tally. Scotland Yard suspected him of two other murders but could not entice him to talk while he was in custody in Singapore. Scripps is suspected of at least one murder in the United States. The case of John Martin Scripps was curious indeed because he began as a very non-violent criminal but then became a grisly serial killer.

SEAN SELLERS

CRIMES?

Sean Sellers was born in Corcoran, California, in 1969. In March, 1986, while still a teenager, Sellers killed his mother and stepfather (Vonda and Lee Bellofatto) in Oklahoma City. The victims were asleep at the time. Sellers crept into their room and shot his step-father. He then shot his mother in the face. Sellers then tried to make the house look like it had been robbed. This ruse obviously didn't work. It later transpired that this wasn't the first time Sellers had murdered someone. In 1985 he shot a convenience store clerk who wouldn't sell him any beer.

Sellers was arrested fairly swiftly for the murders of these relatives. At the trial he said he was a Satanist and had become possessed by a demon. His lawyers tried to give the impression

that he was addicted to Dungeons & Dragons and that this was
a factor in the murders. They were referencing the 'Satanic
panic' rumpus surrounding D&D. Dungeons & Dragons is a
fantasy tabletop role-playing game (RPG) originally designed
by Gary Gygax and Dave Arneson, and first published in 1974.
Over fifty million people around the world have played
Dungeons & Dragons since it was invented in 1974. The game
has though suffered from various controversies in its history.

In 1979, 16-year-old child prodigy James Dallas Egbert III
vanished from his room at Michigan State University. He was
later found in tunnels underneath the university. Egbert, who
had mental health problems, later shot himself. His
disappearance and later death was all (wrongly) blamed on
Dungeons & Dragons. The moral panic over Dungeons &
Dragons got so bizarre in the end there were even stories
about participants in the game seeking to heighten the
experience by having Dungeons & Dragons sessions in caves
and underground catacombs and then vanishing - never to be
seen again. The fact that anyone could think your average
Dungeons & Dragons player was a Devil worshipping occultist
who spent their spare time lurking in caves and catacombs was
preposterous.

The campaign seemed especially misplaced because Gary
Gygax, the co-creator of the game, was a regular at his local
church and as far away from a Satanist as you could get. In
1982, a young man named Irving Pulling shot himself and his
family blamed his obsession with Dungeons & Dragons. An
organisation called B.A.D.D. (Bothered About Dungeons &
Dragons) and conservative Christian groups tried to get the
game banned because they believed it celebrated demonology
and witchcraft. The game was banned from a few school
libraries in America but most people seemed to feel the
campaign against Dungeons & Dragons was absurd. The
legendary FPS video game Doom and the Harry Potter books
would later provoke, to varying degrees, similar moral panics.
Harry Potter is the most banned book in America, according to
the American Library Association. Senior figures in the

Catholic Church accused the Potter books of eroding Christianity.

One would think that the best tactic for Sellers' lawyers would have been to plead insanity rather than waffle on about D&D. Sellers later said himself that Dungeons & Dragons played no part in his crimes. Sellers was found guilty of multiple homicides and sentenced to death in 1986. This was a controversial verdict given the young age of Sean Sellers. The sentence was a result of a quirk in Oklahoma law which did not give juries the option of giving a life sentence without the possibility of parole. They were basically giving the jury two choices. The death penalty OR Sean Sellers probably being released on parole one day while still a relatively young man. The jury evidently felt the latter option was too lenient given the nature of the crimes.

Sean Sellers (as ever with murderers and criminals) found God in prison and said he was no longer a Satanist. He appeared on television shows and became something of a true crime celebrity. There were many appeals against his death sentence and he tried to argue that he suffered from a personality disorder and therefore wasn't of sound mind when he was sentenced. The experts could never quite decide though if Sellers really did have a personality disorder or was simply a very good actor. Sellers was finally executed by lethal injection in 1999. He sang Christian music as his execution loomed. Sellers remains the only person executed in the United States for a crime committed under the age of 17 since the reinstatement of the death penalty in 1976.

LAST MEAL?

Sean Sellers was a rarity when it comes to death row because he had Chinese food as his last meal. He had some egg rolls as part of his meal. Egg rolls are a variety of deep-fried appetisers served in American Chinese restaurants. An egg roll is a cylindrical, savory roll with shredded cabbage, chopped pork, and other fillings inside a thickly-wrapped wheat flour skin, which is fried in hot oil. Sellers also had sweet and sour shrimp. This dish comprises of shrimp cooked in a tangy sauce. Vegetables and peppers are often added. Sellers wasn't quite finished yet because he also had some batter-fried shrimp with his Chinese themed last supper.

TOMMY LEE SELLS

CRIMES?

Tommy Lynn Sells was born in Oakland, California, in 1964. He was connected to around a dozen murders but he claimed to have killed about seventy people. Sells said he simply lost count in the end. He said that killing for him was like taking a shot of dope. It was the ultimate high and he was constantly chasing that high once he'd sampled it.

His first murder is believe to have occurred when he was working at a fair. This was in 1985. A woman from the fair had invited Sells home but then she tried to steal some money from him so he clubbed her to death with a baseball bat. Her ten year-old son was a witness to the murder so Sells murdered the boy too.

Sells is believed to have killed at least seven people in the second part of the 1980s. He was well known to the police and authorities for felony and vehicle theft in the eighties but they were obviously unaware at the time that he was killer too. Sells was essentially a drifter. He worked at fairs and laboured on construction sites. He also stole and cheated to get by. In the early nineties, after another spell in prison, Sells was begging on the street and a kind hearted woman noticed him and said she would get him some food. As she was getting the food, Sells barged into her home and raped her. He then stabbed the woman multiple times.

Incredibly though, he pleaded guilty to malicious wounding and the rape charges were dropped. Sells only served three years in prison for this awful attack. The decision to give Sells such a light sentence turned out to be completely insane. He continued to kill. His victims included 13-year-old Kaylene Harris and 9-year-old Mary Beatrice Perez. Sells was especially sadistic and indiscriminate. He stabbed and strangled children with no remorse or pity.

In 1999, Sells attacked two girls (ages 13 and 10) and slashed their throats. Kaylene Harris was killed but her ten year-old friend Krystal Surles, despite horrendous wounds and a severed trachea, managed to survive and get to some help. A police artist sketch of the suspect matched Tommy Lynn Sells (who was of course, as we have noted, very well known to the police). Sells confessed to the police once in custody and said he had first killed when he was fifteen.

Sells was sentenced to death and executed by lethal injection at Texas State Penitentiary in 2014. Krystal Surles was in the watching audience when he was put to death - as were the family of Kaylene Harris. As far as they were concerned the world was a better place without Tommy Lee Sells and it's hard to argue with them on that. If his claim of killing dozens of people is true than there are many victims of Sells yet to be found. He would kill by any means possible, be it a weapon or his bare hands, and he usually raped the victims before he killed them.

Sells said he had no emotions whatsoever apart from hate and never felt any pity, mercy, or sorrow for victims. He was a complete tabula rasa who found it easy to kill someone in harrowing fashion and then go about his normal day as if nothing had happened. Sells once even killed a heavily pregnant woman and her baby. He did a prison interview before he was executed and came across as a cold, blank, and terrifying man of low intelligence. Tommy Lynn Sells was a brutal and horribly evil man who caused much misery and human suffering in his years on this planet. He was definitely not someone you would ever have wanted to meet.

LAST MEAL?

Texas had abolished the last meal custom by the time that Tommy Lynn Sells was executed. Therefore he was simply offered food that was on the prison menu that day. For his last breakfast before his execution, Sells had a lightish and fairly healthy meal of pancakes, oatmeal and apple juice.

GARY CARL SIMMONS

CRIMES?

Gary Carl Simmons was executed in Mississippi in 2012 for his part in the 1996 murder of 21-year-old Jeffrey Wolfe. Wolfe had visited Simmons with his girlfriend Brook Weber to collect a drug debt. Simmons was with a man named Timothy Milano at the time. Milano was his brother-in-law. Simmons didn't have the drug money and an altercation ensued which ended up with Milano shooting Wolfe dead. Simmons then tied up Wolfe's girlfriend and later raped her. Simmons dismembered Wolfe's body and scattered the remains in a bayou swamp full of alligators. For this crime (which sounds like something out of a Tobe Hooper movie), Simmons was executed by lethal injection.

Gary Carl Simmons was a grocery store butcher - which probably explains why he was so good at dissecting the body. Simmons is believed to have owed Wolfe money for marijuana which amounted to thousands. That was clearly a lot of marijuana! Milano shot Wolfe with a rifle and then Simmons cut the body up in the bath. The body parts of Jeffrey Wolfe were found floating in the water. The police were only able to piece together about 80% of Wolfe's body. It took several days to find the body parts.

Wolfe's girlfriend Brook Weber had been locked in a cupboard after her ordeal but she managed to escape in the end and get to a neighbour's house to ask for help. The police were then alerted. Timothy Milano was arrested in his apartment while Simmons fled to his wife's house but then (for some reason) made a video confession before turning himself in. Milano was also sentenced to death for his part in the murder. It only took about four days for Simmons to be found guilty of all charges at his trial. The charges were kidnapping, rape and capital murder. Simmons declined a sedative before his execution and approached his death in stoic fashion.

LAST MEAL?

Gary Carl Simmons requested one of the more calorific meals in death row history before his execution. He had a Pizza Hut medium Super Supreme Deep Dish pizza. Pizza Hut's Super Supreme Pizza features black olives, ham and Italian sausage, pepperoni, beef, seasoned pork, mushrooms, green bell peppers and onions. Simmons also had a family size bag of nacho cheese Doritos. Doritos is an American brand of flavored tortilla chips produced since 1964 by Frito-Lay, a wholly owned subsidiary of PepsiCo. The original Doritos were not flavoured. Cheese Doritos only came out in 1972.

Gary Carl Simmons also requested a second pizza - which was crammed with toppings that included garlic. He also had 10 8-oz. packs of Parmesan cheese, one super-size order of McDonald's fries, sliced jalapenos, ranch dressing, and jalapeno nacho cheese dip. To wash down this epic junk food binge, Simmons had two cherry cokes and two strawberry milkshakes. For his dessert, Simmons had two pints of strawberry ice cream. His food order came in at 30,000 calories!

Gary Carl Simmons was clearly a big eater because that same day, before his generous last meal, he had meatloaf patty, rice, salad, cornbread, and gravy for lunch. He'd already eaten some eggs for his breakfast. Simmons' mug shots show him to be a hefty man carrying a few extra pounds. He was clearly someone who enjoyed his grub.

RUTH SNYDER

CRIMES?

Ruth Snyder was born in New York in 1895. Along with her lover Henry Judd Gray, she murdered her husband Albert in 1927. Ruth is believed to have grown to hate her husband because he was still obsessed with a deceased fiancee from the past. Albert apparently even had a portrait of this old flame in the house - with Ruth obviously didn't enjoy very much. There were stories too that Albert was a strict sort of husband who treated Ruth quite badly.

Henry and Ruth garroted Albert and stuffed his nose and face with drugged rags. Ruth then told the police there had been a robbery at her house and her husband had been murdered by the thieves. The police immediately got suspicious of this story because there was little sign of a forced entry. Ruth's scam was further blown apart when items she had reported as stolen in the robbery were then found hidden in the house.

Henry Judd Gray also dented the murder scheme when his alibi was proven to be false and his whereabouts the night of the night of the murder became highly suspicious to the police. Ruth and Henry soon ratted on each other in custody and tried to pin the murder on one another. They were both sentenced to death and ended up in the electric chair. They were executed ten minutes apart at Sing Sing in Ossining, New York. This murder case was the inspiration for the famous film Double Indemnity. Ruth's execution was photographed by a Chicago Tribune photographer. A famous photo of her in the electric chair looks like something out of one of the Saw movies.

LAST MEAL?

Ruth Snyder had chicken parmesan as part of her last meal.
Chicken parmigiana, or chicken parmesan is a dish of breaded
chicken breast covered in tomato sauce and mozzarella,
parmesan, or provolone cheese. With this she had some
Alfredo Pasta. Alfredo Pasta is an Italian pasta dish made
using fresh pasta, vegetables, chicken pieces combined with
butter, cream and cheese. A very Italian last supper then for
Ruth Snyder.

Ruth had ice cream and two milkshakes for dessert. That must
have been quite a sugar rush. Ruth washed this all down with
grape soda. Grape soda first appeared as a variety of
carbonated drink provided in soda fountains in American
drugstores in the late nineteenth century.

FRANK SPISAK

CRIMES?

Frank Spisak was born in 1951. Spisak was a lunatic with a
Hitler toothbrush mustache who committed three racially
motivated murders in 1982. He was a transvestite who wanted
to have a sex change operation but then changed his mind. He
no longer wanted to become a woman anymore. He NOW
wanted to become Adolf Hitler. Spisak's first victim was 57
year old black minister Rev. Horace Rickerson. This murder
took place at Cleveland State University. Spisak had wandered
onto the campus with a gun looking for a black person to
shoot. A few months later, Spisak shot John Hardaway on a
transit platform. Hardaway (thankfully) survived and was later
able to testify against Spisak in court.

A few months later Spisak tried to shoot Coletta Dartt at the
Cleveland State University but (thankfully again) missed the

target. Coletta, like John Hardaway, was therefore able to be a witness against Spisak when he was captured. A few weeks later, 50 year old Timothy Sheehan was found shot to death at Cleveland State University. Spisak later said he had shot Sheehan because he suspected the victim might be Jewish. Only a few days later, Spisak shot a student named Brian Warford.

Frank Spisak was then arrested for shooting his gun out of his apartment window. At the time the police had no idea he was the maniac responsible for these local shootings. They only deduced this when they checked the gun and found it matched the weapon used on the local people who had been shot recently. Frank Spisak pleaded insanity at his trial. He certainly looked and sounded insane but nonetheless he was given a death sentence and finally executed by lethal injection in Ohio in 2011.

Spisak hadn't done himself too many favours in court by giving the Nazi salute each time he entered. When he was called to give evidence he started waffling on about how the Jews were created by Satan. He seemed amused in court when he reflected on the murders and said he felt like he had finally done something 'constructive' with his life by killing black people.

Frank Spisak seemed to enjoy the five minutes of dark fame afforded to him by the trial. He played up to the gallery and had prickly sarcastic exchanges with the prosecutor. The trial became darkly comic because Spisak insisted that his legal team should call him Frances. In his last statement before he was put to death, Frank Spisak read from the Bible in German. Suffice to say, he was a very troubled and highly dangerous man.

When he was in prison long after the trial, Frank Spisak told a parole board that he was no longer a Nazi. Well, it was a bit late for that. The damage had already been done. Spisak was so crazy that even neo-Nazi groups in the area were quick to distance themselves from him and said he had nothing to do with them. Spisak was really just a loner with mental health issues. These mental health issues manifested themselves in the most tragic circumstances imaginable. His legal team, not unreasonably, argued that it was barbaric to execute people with mental illness but these appeals fell on deaf ears. Spisak's execution was Ohio's last execution using the drug sodium thiopental.

LAST MEAL?

Frank Spisak went for a fairly modest and simple last meal on death row. He had spaghetti in a light tomato sauce. It is probably no coincidence at all that this is the last thing Hitler ate too. Spisak also had some salad in Italian dressing. For his afters he chose chocolate cake. Chocolate cake is quite popular on death row. His meal was washed down with root beer and coffee. Trivia you will never need - Hitler's distinctive toothbrush mustache is alleged to have originated from his service in the First World War. It is speculated that Hitler had to trim his (more traditional) mustache to wear a gas mask.

JOSEPH STALIN

CRIMES?

Joseph Stalin (1878–1953) was the leader of the Soviet Union during the war and had held this position from the mid-twenties. When it comes to statistics, Stalin was an even more prolific mass murderer than Hitler. Stalin sent millions to their deaths in labour camps (Gulags). He was a ruthless and heartless man. Born in present day Georgia, Stalin was from a poor background and a political agitator as a young man. In 1912, Lenin, then in exile in Switzerland, appointed Stalin to serve on the first Central Committee of the Bolshevik Party. After Lenin died in 1924, Stalin eventually outmanoeuvred his rivals and won the power struggle for control of the Communist Party. By the late 1920s, he had become dictator of the Soviet Union. Stalin was ruthless and ruled by fear. His ambition was to transform the Soviet Union into an industrial and military superpower.

Stalin was of course pivotal to the war and a darkly fascinating presence at the heart of the storm. He was Machiavellian and sinister. After his merciless purges (Stalin murdered most of the army's officers before the war lest they should conspire against him), Stalin refashioned the Red Army as his own creature with the command based around those associated with the First Cavalry Army that had been raised during the civil war. The First Cavalry Army had sided with Stalin during his struggles with Trotsky and First Cavalry Army men like Budenny and Voroshilov are rewarded with prime positions in the new military structure.

Gradually, control freak Stalin loosened his grip though and learned to trust the most competent (Zhukov, Konev, Rokossovsky etc) of the brand new officer corps that emerged - even if he had no personal connection to them. A new cadre of Soviet generals found themselves and provided the Red Army with the organisation and leadership it so desperately needed. This is fundamental to the changing fortunes of the Soviet Union through the course of the war.

Stalin was a victim of his own hubris early on. Convinced that he can avoid war with Germany (at least until such a point that the Soviet Union will be better prepared) with politics and his own presumed cunning (the noxious Nazi-Soviet pact), Stalin almost enters a state of denial and unreality when the Wehrmacht rolls forward across the Soviet frontier on Midsummer's Day, 1941. The Soviet dictator had ignored many warnings that the Germans were about to attack. They came from his spy network, generals and of course Britain and the United States. It seemed to be the worst kept secret in the world that Hitler intended to smash the Soviet Union.

So the early disasters were Stalin's fault as much as anyone but he was quick to resort to revisionism to mask this early crisis. When the fortunes of the Soviet Union improved and they eventually won the war, he claimed it was all because of his firm leadership and collective industrial policies. The early blunders were brushed under the Kremlin carpet.

One important change comes in the way that the Red Army is hamstrung by military commissars and secret police. These political officers are placed within the army by party and state because Stalin (like all dictators and their military apparatus) is absolutely paranoid about losing control of the Red Army. The political officers are often incompetent and also suspicious of the Red Army, creating fractious and strained relationships at every turn. They complicate and confuse the command structure.

Stalin - despite his natural instincts - is well aware of this and in 1942 changes the structure of the army. A new cadre of talented (if brutal) generals comes to prominence as the German invasion loses momentum and Stalin gives them more freedom of action. Perhaps the most extraordinary feat of the Soviet system is the evacuation of factories and heavy industry to the east through total manpower mobilisation. Stalin, through more interaction with his generals, learns the important lesson that space can be traded for time. With the evacuated industries they eventually produce tanks, planes and guns on a level far beyond the Germans.

Stalin would never visit the front and more or less stayed in Moscow, even when it appeared to be in danger of attack. His generals and soldiers always felt his presence though, however far away he was. Stalin was always on the telephone and would also dispatch some very sardonic and laced telegrams to any general he felt was not performing as he should do. If you were a hapless Red Army general in the early days of the war when the Germans were destroying everything in their path, your prospects of a long life were not that great because even if you somehow escaped German encirclement or capture, Stalin was waiting to pronounce his own judgement.

Although Stalin never visited his soldiers they too felt his presence through the course of the conflict. A key weapon of Stalin besides propaganda in control of the mass of the army was fear. The ruthless NKVD squads treated lost soldiers as if they were deserters and shot them out of hand. The regular army included penal battalions who were used to clear minefields and when these men were liberated in their thousands at the end of the war they were often sent to detention camps by Stalin for the high crime of having been captured by the Germans.

Then there were the "guards" armies, more elite and professional formations. The professional upgrade of the army and the return of gold braid, medals etc, was a clear sign that Stalin had bungled the conception of the army at first and was now reversing his previous approach. He was a thug and a mass murderer and made more mistakes than he would ever admit to but ultimately he proved to be a shrewd, ruthless and able war leader. Stalin died in 1953.

LAST MEAL?

Stalin attended one last dinner with his inner circle before his death. It was the usual banquet style meal with fish, bread, desserts and all sorts of stuff. Stalin enjoyed meat dishes and he liked strong cheese and pickled cheese. He was also fond of dried fruits and a big fan of soup. Those who knew Stalin said he also had fish on the menu quite often. Stalin liked Stroganina. This is a dish made of raw sliced fish. You could describe it as an acquired taste. Stalin absolutely loved bananas because they were considered to be a luxury in the Soviet Union at the time. Stalin was a big drinker and always had numerous types of brandy, wine, and vodka available at the dinner table. Stalin and Churchill are said to have had some very boozy meetings during the war.

GERALD STANO

CRIMES?

Gerald Stano was born in New York in 1950. He was born Paul Zeininger and suffered neglect at the hands of his biological mother. He was put up for adoption and got his name when a nurse named Norma Stano adopted him. He only graduated from high school when he was 21. He could never hold down a job as an adult and was a compulsive thief and liar. In the end he moved in with his adopted parents in Florida.

Stano claimed to have begun his murder spree in the late 1960s although it is more verifiable that he became a serial killer in the early 1970s. He claimed to have killed over forty women. Twenty-two murders are verified. Gerald Stano said that, to him, killing a human being was like stepping on a bug. He killed by any means possible but never raped the victims. His victims were found to have multiple stab wounds suggestive of a frenzied and gruesome attack both before and after death. His youngest victim was thirteen.

Aside from stabbing, he choked other victims to death and sometimes used a gun. Stano said he killed six women in Pennsylvania but the vast majority of his murders took place in Florida. Stano always felt like an outcast in society and this, combined with his low intelligence and obvious sadistic streak, clearly tilted him over the edge. It is said that Stano had an addiction to drugs and alcohol. In the 1970s he actually got married and tried to stop drinking but this attempt to get his life back to some semblance of normality obviously didn't last. The marriage lasted six months and his wife cited abuse as the reason for the separation.

In 1980, a prostitute named Donna Hensley went to the police and said that a man she met had just tried to 'slice' her up with a knife. She demanded that the police find this man and charge him before he tried to hurt anyone else. The police investigated the incident and eventually discovered that the car and licence plate the woman described belonged to 29 year-old Gerald Stano.

The police noticed that Stano had a long arrest sheet. They were also investigating a number of murders and disappearances in the area. Under questioning, Stano cracked and confessed to murder. He told the police he had murdered 40 women. Stano was found guilty of nine murders and received eight life sentences and one death sentence. Stano was housed with Ted Bundy when he was in prison in the early eighties. He was killed by electric chair in 1998 in Florida State Prison.

LAST MEAL?

For his last meal Stano asked for steak and a (you guessed it) baked potato. He also requested a salad with blue cheese dressing. Blue cheese dressing is a salad dressing and usually made of some combination of blue cheese, mayonnaise, and buttermilk, sour cream or yogurt, milk, vinegar, onion powder, and garlic powder. That was a fairly healthy main course when it come to death row last suppers.

Lima beans are also believed to have been part of Stano's last meal. These are a lot like butter beans and have excellent health benefits (not that Stano need worry about such things by now). For his dessert, Stano had mint chocolate chip ice cream. As we've noted, mint chocolate chip ice cream tends not to be hugely popular compared to other ice cream flavours like chocolate and vanilla. Maybe this is because mint chocolate chip ice cream is not a natural side dish to something like a fruit pie? It is too distinctive and best eaten on its own. If you have a nice fruit pie you don't want it to be overwhelmed by mint. Stano's meal was washed down with a generous amount of Pepsi.

JOSEPH TABORSKY

CRIMES?

Joseph "Mad Dog" Taborsky was a killer who left several people dead after a spate of violent robberies. He was killed by electric chair in 1960. He was born in Connecticut in 1924. Taborsky would rob stores and off licences. He got his nickname from the brutal methods he employed while robbing and thieving. He would pistol whip victims and - as his victim tally obviously suggests - wasn't afraid to shoot people. He had a low IQ and was clearly completely crazy too.

Taborsky was pretty weird in that he was on death row twice. He was released from his first stint in prison but inevitably ended up back there when he returned to his old ways. He was 37 years-old at the time of his death. Taborsky's case was also weird in that his brother, something of a criminal accomplice by all accounts, once testified against him in court to get a lesser charge. The first time he was released from prison, Taborsky told the authorities he would now keep his nose clean and wouldn't get so much as a parking ticket in the future. Sadly, this turned out to be one the least truthful statements in human history.

It was after this that Taborsky began what you might describe as his grocery store rampages. His accomplice for many of these was another ex-con named Arthur "Meatball" Culombe. Despite all the murders, what really got Taborsky into big trouble was an incident where he beat two elderly grocery store owners unconscious but then noticed that their three year-old granddaughter was still in the store running around playing. Taborsky ordered Culombe to shoot the little girl.

Culombe had a heart though (a BIT of a heart - he clearly wasn't too bothered about old people being beaten up) and when Taborksy left the store he told the girl to hide and shot into the floor. Taborksy was therefore fooled into thinking the girl was dead. There's no doubt that Taborksy wanted the girl dead and probably would have shot her himself if he'd known she'd survived. Heartless indeed. When the pair were arrested, Culombe's actions in saving the little girl spared him from the electric chair. He was given life in prison instead. Culombe, in an otherwise wretched life, had at least done one good and decent thing.

Culombe was seen as very much the junior partner in this crime duo. All the evidence suggested that he was dominated by Taborsky. Culombe was also pretty cooperative with the authorities too - which doubtless further helped him avoid a death sentence. There was no such fortune for Joseph "Mad Dog" Taborsky. His luck had finally run out. Taborsky is generally credited with seven victims but as ever with serial murderers the true victim tally might be higher. I'd imagine that many grocery store owners breathed a heavy sigh of relief when they learned that "Mad Dog" Taborsky was in custody and behind bars.

LAST MEAL?

Taborsky's last meal request was fairly simple as far as last meal requests go. He skipped the main course and went straight to dessert. As far as food goes he only asked for a banana split. There are variations of this dish but it is basically a banana served with ice cream and a chocolate sauce. Whipped cream is added and usually some crushed nuts are sprinkled on the top. It is traditional to add cherries to the top too and if you really want to throw the boat out you can add some wafers. The banana split is believed to have originated in the United States. Most sources cite its creator as David "Doc" Strickler. In 1904 Strickler came up with this banana themed dessert and charged ten cents for it.

As we've seen, quite a few death row inmates have requested a banana split as part of their last meal. What makes this dish work is the fact that bananas and chocolate go well together.

In Britain an old traditional working-class comfort food used to be bananas and custard. I'm not sure if anyone still eats bananas and custard but it's surprisingly good. Taborsky clearly had a sweet tooth because he washed down his banana split with cherry soda. He also had a cup of coffee with BOTH sugar and cream.

KARLA FAYE TUCKER

CRIMES?

Karla Faye Tucker was born in Houston in 1959. Tucker was convicted of two murders in Texas in 1984 and executed by lethal injection after fourteen years on death row. She was convicted for killing two people with a pickaxe during a burglary. Tucker had a very unconventional and damaging childhood. Her mother was a rock groupie who got Karla involved in prostitution when she was only thirteen. Karla also began drinking and taking drugs at a preposterously young age. Her father left home when she was very young so she had no role models in her life whatsoever. When Karla was only twenty her mother died of a drugs overdose and left her feeling alone in the world.

In the early eighties, Karla (then still in her early twenties) spent most of her time with a biker gang and on June the 13th, 1983, Karla and a man named Daniel Ryan Garrett went to the Houston apartment of Jerry Lynn Dean. Karla and Garrett were both off their heads on a variety of drugs and much alcohol. The purpose of their visit was to steal Dean's motorcycle. Dean was the former husband of Karla's best friend and Karla seemed to have a dislike for him (it is said that Dean once destroyed some photographs of Karla's mother).

Jerry Lynn Dean was sleeping when they entered the

apartment so Garrett hit him with a hammer. Karla Faye Tucker then finished Dean off by striking him with a pickaxe. The duo then noticed that someone else was in the room. This turned out to be a young woman named Deborah Thornton. Karla attacked Deborah with the pickaxe and struck her several times. Deborah was left dead with the pickaxe still lodged in her body. Karla and Garrett then stole some money and fled. In the space of a few minutes Karla Faye Tucker had brutally slaughtered two people with a pickaxe. She was later recorded on a police wire tap saying that she'd experienced an orgasm each time she'd struck one of the victims with the pickaxe.

The police investigation didn't take too long to deduce that Karla and Garrett were the culprits for this gruesome crime and they were brought into custody in a matter of weeks. Karla Faye Tucker and Daniel Ryan Garrett were both sentenced to death at the trial which followed (Karla had been advised by her legal team to plead not guilty - which was obviously a mistake). Karla said she didn't even remember that night because she had taken so many drugs. Garrett died of liver disease in 1993 before he could be executed.

Karla Faye Tucker, meanwhile, found God while in prison and a campaign to have her death sentence commuted attracted support from various people and groups including Pope John Paul II, Newt Gingrich, Bianca Jagger, and the European Parliament. Why all the sympathy for a woman who had brutally killed two innocent people with a pickaxe? If you were being really cynical you might suggest it was because Karla was female, white, and quite attractive. These famous campaigners didn't seem to be offering the same sympathy and support to black male prisoners on death row for similar violent crimes.

Still, it was hard not to at least have some degree of sympathy for Karla. She didn't seem like a monster at all and while most killers conveniently seem to find God in prison she appeared more sincere than most. Karla wrote a long letter to Texas

Governor George W. Bush in which she asked to have her death sentence commuted and expressed her sorrow for what she had done. Karla said she would help rehabilitate other women in prison so that they were better people when they were released. Bush predictably (and rather heartlessly you might suggest) simply ignored this letter and refused to get involved. He didn't really care if a woman was executed or not. Bush had voters to think about and didn't want to be seen to be being weak on crime. Karla Faye Tucker was therefore executed by lethal injection on February the 3rd, 1998.

LAST MEAL?

Karla Faye Tucker had a very basic and simple last meal. She requested a banana, a peach, and a garden salad with ranch dressing. A garden salad is a a type of tossed green salad made with lettuce (usually a blend including mostly iceberg lettuce.) It usually carrots, tomatoes, cucumbers and onions. Croutons are often added to this salad for some extra crunch and texture. Ranch dressing is an American salad dressing usually made from buttermilk, salt, garlic, onion, mustard, herbs, and spices mixed into a sauce based on mayonnaise. Karla was evidently not very interested in food at this time. It is said that, despite the frugal nature of her last meal, she didn't even eat much of it.

ROBERT VAN HOOK

CRIMES?

Robert Van Hook was born in Sharonville, Ohio in 1960. In 1985, Hook went to a gay bar in Cincinnati and ended up going home with a 25 year-old man named David Self. Hook was also 25 at the time. Once they got to Self's apartment, Van Hook eventually strangled Self and then repeatedly stabbed him. Once the victim was dead, Van Hook ransacked the apartment and left with some jewelry and a leather jacket he'd found. Hook later said that he'd been robbing gay men since he was a teenager. He saw them as easy targets.

In this, Van Hook was similar to a British killer named Colin Ireland. Ireland would pick up men in pubs and go home with them. Then he would restrain, murder, and rob them. On the 20th of August 1993, at the Old Bailey, Ireland was sentenced to life imprisonment for five murders of gay men. Colin Ireland said that he wasn't gay and simply picked on gay men because they were easy targets. There was certainly some similarity in these two case on opposite sides of the ocean.

Van Hook's murder of David self was brutal. He stabbed the victim so heavily the blade entered the brain. Van Hook then tried to cut the head off. He also gutted the victim. Van Hook also left a cigarette butt inside one the wounds. There was evidence that Self's internal organs had been stabbed. Van Hook fled to Fort Lauderdale, Florida after the murder. He later said that gay men were usually too frightened to report being robbed and this was why they made such good targets. If this was the case though it didn't really explain he'd blown a gasket and brutally murdered poor David Self.

Van Hook had served in the military previously. He said he'd had an abusive childhood and was suffering from severe mental health issues and PTSD at the time of the murder. He was arrested about a month after the death of David Self. There was enough forensic evidence to connect Van Hook to the crime. His lawyers tried an interesting but doomed tactic in court. They argued that Van Hook suffered from 'homosexual panic' because he couldn't deal with his repressed sexual desires. What they hoped to gain from this strange defence is anyone's guess. It hardly explained or mitigated the death and mutilation of David Self.

Van Hook confessed to the murder and tried to plead insanity but he was sentenced to death. As usual, a long period of legal to and throw began as his legal team tried to avoid the execution going ahead. Van Hook turned out to be pretty violent in prison too and was involved in an incident where he stabbed another inmate. The execution of Robert Van Hook took place on July the 18th, 2018, at the Southern Ohio Correctional Facility in Lucasville, Ohio.

Van hook's execution was quite controversial and made local headlines because at the time Ohio's lawmakers were trying to phase out and ban the use of the lethal injections for executions. This debate all came slightly too late for Van Hook. Before he was executed he offered an apology to the family of David Self. One of Van Hook's lawyers later admitted this apology was probably less than sincere since Van Hook had never expressed any remorse at all for Self or the murder while in prison.

LAST MEAL?

For his last meal, Robert Van Hook had a simple guilty pleasure sort of blowout. His main course was double cheeseburgers and French fries. For his dessert he had strawberry cheesecake with whipped cream and a vanilla milkshake. The only unusual thing on Van Hook's list of last meal requests was the beverage he chose to wash down this food. Van Hook had some grapefruit juice. That was certainly rare and something different from the usual Coke or Dr Pepper.

CHESTER WICKER

CRIMES?

Chester Wicker was born in 1943. On April the 4th, 1980, he abducted Suzanne Knuth in Galveston. Knuth had been out with her husband that night but when their car broke down she decided to walk home while he waited for someone to come out and fix the car. Tragically this turned out to be a big mistake because she ran into Chester Wicker. Wicker saw the woman walking down the road and swung his car around. He then forced her into the vehicle.

Wicker raped and strangled Knuth and buried her alive. Her body was only found nearly three weeks later. Knuth was a 22 year-old university librarian. She had been choked unconscious and buried in sand. Chester Wicker immediately became suspicious to his family after the murder. His uncle had noticed blood in his car and on his shirt when he saw him. Chester Wicker's explanations for this were not even convincing to his relatives let alone the police (who quickly zeroed in on Wicker). He was arrested just over two weeks after the murder and had no option but to confess and show detectives where the body was buried.

Chester Wicker was no stranger to the police and the criminal system. In 1971 he had been sentenced to ten years in prison for rape but got out on parole after a couple of years. In 1973 he was charged with attempted rape and served another prison stretch. It was probably inevitable that he was going to end up back in prison for good one day.

It was an awful case. Wicker was always a bad egg. Wicker's legal team worked hard to avoid the death penalty and earned him two reprieves on death row. He wasn't so lucky the third time around. Wicker was executed by lethal injection in Texas on August the 26th, 1986.

LAST MEAL?

Wicker's last meal must rank as one of the most straight forward and simple requests when it comes to condemned prisoners. All he had was some lettuce and tomatoes. He washed this skimpy (if healthy) meal down with two glasses of milk.

STEVEN MICHAEL WOODS

CRIMES?

Steven Michael Woods Jr. was born in Texas in 1980. Woods was implicated in the murders of Ronald Whitehead, 21, and Bethena Brosz, 19, in 2001 in north Texas. The general gist is that Rhodes and Woods were alleged to have lured the victims to their doom by pretending that were offering a drugs transaction. The thing is though, that it was Woods' co-defendant, Marcus Rhodes, who shot the victims. Woods was basically done on charges of aiding and abetting. He didn't kill the victims but was still sentenced to death.

The victims were shot and then had their throats cut. The possessions of the victims were later found in the car belonging to Rhodes. Woods said he had spent the evening with the victims the night before. Some of the witnesses at the trial said that Woods had bragged about planning to kill them. He vehemently denied this though. After the murders Woods had initially fled and was arrested soon after. Woods argued that all he did was run for his life after being the witness to a savage murder.

Steven Michael Woods Jr was ultimately doomed by a feature of Texas law which states that you don't have to have fired the fatal bullet to be convicted of murder. If you are an accomplice to murder or showed a disregard for human life (presumably this means you did nothing to stop the murder) then you can be treated as a murderer under the law of the state. As you might imagine, the interpretation of this law and its application to this specific criminal case was knotty, complex, and controversial to say the least.

The general explanation of this case is that the law ultimately decided that Woods had some degree of participation in the planning of this murder. Rhodes, who pled guilty, actually got treated with more leniency. The death sentence handed to Woods was seen as a travesty of justice to many - not least Woods himself. Amnesty International in particular were highly critical of the case. Woods was rather unlucky to be tried in Texas - a state that isn't squeamish when it comes to executing criminals. Before his execution by lethal injection in 2011, Woods made a speech in which he declared that this was not an execution but a murder.

LAST MEAL?

Woods certainly couldn't be accused of going for a prosaic or simple last meal. He requested a table shuddering epic as his last supper. He had two pounds of bacon to begin with and then asked for no less than four pizzas. He also had fried chicken steaks and some chicken breast. Woods definitely wasn't finished yet though because he also had two hamburgers. As a side dish to this gargantuan supper he had French fries and garlic bread sticks.

For his dessert he had two pints of ice cream. To wash down this hearty feast he had sweet tea, Pepsi, root beer, and Mountain Dew. Root beer is a carbonated soft drink. Its main flavour ingredient is sarsaparilla root. Mountain Dew, stylized as Mtn Dew, is a carbonated soft drink brand produced and owned by PepsiCo. The original formula was invented in 1940 by Tennessee beverage bottlers Barney and Ally Hartman.

AILEEN WUORNOS

CRIMES?

Aileen Wuornos was born in Rochester, Michigan, in 1956. Aileen Wuornos is arguably the most famous female serial killer thanks to a film and documentary which ere made about her crimes. She killed seven men in total from 1989 to 1990.

Wuornos had an abusive upbringing at the hands of a strict grandfather. Wuornos was a surprisingly beautiful child but a tough life obviously extracted a cruel toll on her looks in the end. She was homeless at fifteen and sold her body to survive. Tired of the cold, she eventually hitchhiked to Florida and married a rich man. The marriage only lasted days. He put a restraining order on her because Wuornos would beat him up.

Aileen Wuornos was a notoriously volatile person with an unpredictable (and rather frightening) temper. After her marriage collapsed, Aileen Wuornos worked as a prostitute and, in desperate need of money, turned to murder. She picked up her victims on the I-75 highway. She would always target middle-aged men in nice cars. Wuornos would start to undress in the car and ask the driver to pull over somewhere secluded. Then she would get out of the car and shoot them before stealing their wallets. Aileen Wuornos would often shoot her victims multiple times. Her alleged motivation for the murders was that she wanted to support her girlfriend and lover Ty. One might argue that a hatred of men was rather evident too.

Psychologist Marissa Harrison concluded from her study that female serial killers were mostly motivated by material gain whereas male serial killers were mostly motivated by sexual urges. Aileen Wuornos was clearly motivated by her desperate desire to get quick money. Wuornos never really did much to hide the bodies of the victims. They were found fairly quickly and easily. A few men had a lucky escape from Aileen Wuornos. One man actually saw the gun in her purse and managed to drive away. Aileen Wuornos was captured when the police finally managed to get an accurate artists impression of the killer. Once this sketch was circulated, they soon had a lot of calls telling them the illustration looked like Aileen Wuornos - an angry and violent local woman who seemed to spend most of her time drinking beer in biker bars.

Wuornos was taken into custody and the police discovered that she had sold the belongings (like wristwatches and jewelry) of the victims in local pawn shops. Any money they had she of course kept for herself. Aileen Wuornos claimed that she had killed the men in self-defence because they all tried to rape her. This was seen as a weak and improbable defence. It appeared unlikely that seven different men all tried to rape her at different times on the exact same stretch of highway. One of the victims was selling Bibles and another was a former police chief. They were ordinary people with no criminal history.

The fact that Wuornos had not reported a single one of these incidents and always tried to hide the bodies also made her defence seem less than plausible. Aileen Wuornos eventually pleaded guilty to five murders because she wanted the death penalty. She was tired of prison and court. Aileen Wuornos felt betrayed and alone in the end. Even her beloved girlfriend Ty secretly taped their phone conversations and testified against her. Wuornos became a born again Christian after her conviction. She always got offended when someone called her a serial killer.

Aileen Wuornos claimed she was not a serial killer because she never tortured or mutilated her victims. While this was true she did shoot dead several innocent men! Aileen Wuornos was executed in 2002. Wuornos declined a last meal before her execution and asked for black coffee. For $15 on crime collectible websites you can buy a photograph of Aileen Wuornos posing with a friend before her execution. She looks surprisingly happy in the photo considering the circumstances in which it was taken. Aileen Wuornos was a twist on the common serial killer situation in that she was a prostitute but a killer rather than a victim. She said she wasn't evil but just had a consuming hatred for the human race.

LAST MEAL?

Not all killers accept a last meal. Aileen Wuornos declined a last meal before her execution and simply asked for some black coffee. She apparently had a couple of burgers earlier in

the day though. Maybe she just wasn't hungry anymore after
eating the burgers.